How To Find Your Soulmate

The Comprehensive Manual For Women Seeking To Discover The Ideal, And Affectionate Gentleman For A Lifelong Partnership

(Practical Tips To Find And Maintain Your Ultimate Love)

Detlef Schilcher

TABLE OF CONTENT

Ensure Your Own Health! 1

Identify Shared Interests And Attributes 63

Striving To Find The Ideal Life Partner 69

Cease Forming Opinions Based On Movies Or Books. 83

Discovering Your Compatible Partner: Criteria To Consider When Searching For A Prospective Life Companion 108

Cease Your Search For Someone To Love You And Instead Focus On Cultivating Self-Love. 117

Love Yourself Unconditionally 162

Ensure Your Own Health!

The paramount counsel for causing someone to develop feelings of love towards you is to prioritize self-love. Consequently, the vast majority of guidance pertaining to relationships encourages the initial emphasis on self-growth and self-care. Acquire that novel expertise and forge additional avenues towards personal growth, cultivate exposure to diverse encounters such as exploration and cultivate a captivating demeanor, consistently push the boundaries of your capabilities and foster the evolution of your character, place a premium on maintaining proper sanitation practices, subsequently enhancing your appeal.

Possessing a genuine self-identity is the most alluring characteristic one can possess. There is no necessity to exhibit pride or arrogance; rather, endeavor to prioritize the cultivation of your mental and physical wellbeing in order to enhance your self-assurance and self-regard. It is essential to foster self-love, as only then can you extend affection towards others and elicit reciprocal sentiments.

The following point holds great significance and should be closely monitored. Due to your inherent benevolence, individuals are susceptible to developing an affectionate fondness for you. While individuals may be initially drawn based on external appearance, it is imperative to note that this factor alone does not suffice.

Engage in benevolent actions, demonstrate compassion towards others, and exhibit kindness towards others. The utmost splendor lies in the profound beauty of your heart and soul.

CHAPTER ONE

DETERMINING GENUINE AFFECTION
The Essence of Love and Its Contrary Notions

The notion of genuine love has been the subject of discussion throughout history.

Skeptics commonly assert its nonexistence, while ardent idealists advocate for the pursuit of finding one's soulmate. With recent scientific validation establishing that genuine love is not only attainable but also capable of enduring indefinitely, we have opted to examine the psychological factors that facilitate the thriving or deterioration of love.

To commence, let us establish a distinct understanding of the essence of genuine love:
In order to determine if one has indeed encountered genuine love, it is imperative to initially apprehend the essential components encompassed within authentic love. In essence, the concept of pure love revolves around possessing an unwavering, indomitable, and unparalleled ardor and loyalty towards one's romantic partner. It is further distinguished by a profound and enduring emotional bond, as well as a physical affinity with one's partner, such

that envisioning life without them is exceedingly difficult to comprehend.

Love possesses dynamism and requires proactive measures for its flourishing. Frequently, we squander our time contemplating our spouse's perception of us or the impression our relationship conveys to others. Although it is delightful to receive love from someone else, we must recognize that each individual can only truly experience their own affection towards another, rather than the reciprocation of those feelings. In order to establish a profound connection with and cultivate tender emotions within ourselves, it is imperative that we engage in compassionate actions. Alternatively, if that is not the case, we may find ourselves residing in a realm of imagination.

Occasionally, it may produce a sense of annoyance, but it is simultaneously quite empowering to acknowledge the notion that our capacity for meaningful impact within a relationship is solely restricted to ourselves. We exercise authority over the aspects within our influence. Hence, we have the option to engage in behaviors that undermine intimacy or to engage in actions that embody emotions such as love, empathy, tenderness, admiration, and benevolence. To intentionally and persistently

Researchers developed a tool known as the "Couples Interactions Chart" in order to evaluate and contrast the characteristics of an ideal partnership with a phenomenon referred to as a "fantasy bond." This fantasy bond can be described as a deceptive perception of connection and closeness that allows couples to maintain a façade of love and affection while keeping an emotional detachment. A fantasy bond is formed when individuals replace genuine love and intimacy with the mere appearance of being in a relationship. This hyperlink diminishes the perceptions of vitality and allure within interpersonal interactions.

Distinguishing Attributes of Genuine Love Compared to a Fantasy Bond

1. Non-defensiveness and openness vs. furious responses to criticism

Key attributes of an affectionate partnership

In order to foster a sense of intimacy, it is important for partners to maintain an openness and receptiveness towards one another, without becoming defensive or disheartening when receiving feedback. Partners are encouraged to diligently search for the essence of truth in their spouse's statements. That particular piece of information could potentially offer a substantial indication as to how we may be unintentionally causing our spouse to detach themselves from us. Despite any disagreements we may have, actively listening to our spouses inherently fosters a sense of acknowledgement, understanding, and compassion within them. Conversely, if we penalize our spouse for displaying honesty and transparency, it effectively hinders the flow of communication.

2. Receptive to engaging in novel experiences. closed to new experiences

A successful partnership arises when both individuals maintain a strong connection with their dynamic, receptive, and authentic aspects, allowing for the embrace of novel encounters. We need not necessarily feel a profound adoration for and actively participate in every pursuit that our spouse cherishes, but by jointly exploring new interests, venturing to unfamiliar places, and regularly challenging customary practices, we infuse renewed vitality into a relationship that invigorates both individuals involved.

3. Honesty and integrity vs. dishonesty and duplicity

To be truthful is among the primary principles instilled in most individuals during their early years. However, in the context of adulthood, it is plausible that a significant amount of deceit exists within the relationships we hold closest to us. Engaging in deceit with our spouse inflicts substantial damage upon them, the relationship itself, and our own well-being. In order to experience a sense of vulnerability with our spouses, it is imperative to establish trust, which can solely be achieved through the practice of honesty.

4. Adherence to the boundaries, aspirations, and objectives of the other party in question, as opposed to. overstepping boundaries

In order to avoid establishing a connection based on fiction, it is essential to regard the other individual as separate from our own selves. This requires regarding them as unique entities, separate and autonomous individuals. Frequently, couples tend to adopt specific roles or conform to power dynamics. We can provide guidance to each other regarding actions and conduct. Alternatively, we may engage in conversations that impose limitations or establish boundaries upon each other. Fundamentally, we perceive them as mere extensions of our own selves rather than regarding them as distinct individuals. Therefore, we limit our affinity towards them. We consider the other individual to be an indispensable asset. We are equally indifferent towards them as we are towards our right arm.

5. The juxtaposition of physical affection and individual sexual identity versus. insufficiency of emotional attachment and the presence of impersonal or monotonous sexual interactions

Expressions of love frequently include the important element of affection in our communication. When we choose to isolate ourselves from our affectionate emotions, we have a tendency to diminish the bond. This diminishes the spark in the dynamics between us and our companions. Sexuality has the potential to lose its significance or personal nature, resulting in a sense of detachment and diminished satisfaction for both individuals involved. Sustaining the presence of love necessitates staying connected to a facet within ourselves that cherishes tactile interaction and is keenly inclined to both give and receive expressions of tenderness.

6. Understanding vs. Misunderstanding occurs when we effortlessly project our own thoughts and assumptions onto our spouse, often leading to misinterpretation of their words. This can happen when we inadvertently utilize their statements as a means to feel hurt or attacked, based on past experiences that resonate with us. It is equally easy to become ensnared in our own perspective, thereby neglecting to consider the vantage point of the other party. We will perpetually remain as two distinct individuals with independent thoughts, consequently, it is unrealistic to expect perfect agreement at all times. Nevertheless, it is imperative to make a concerted effort to perceive our partner from a lucid perspective. When our partner experiences the perception of

being acknowledged and comprehended, they exhibit a greater inclination to empathize and grasp our perspective.

7. Actions that are not controlling, manipulative, or threatening in nature. exploitation of power dynamics
Numerous couples encounter dynamics wherein one party assumes a parental role while the other adopts a more childlike demeanor.
the-fantasy-bond
An individual seeks counsel from the other party, only to later harbor resentment towards that party for offering guidance. Alternatively, an individual endeavors to govern the situation and subsequently asserts that the other party is exhibiting traits of irresponsibility, immaturity, or passiveness. For a relationship to be characterized by love, it is essential that there is a fair distribution of benefits and responsibilities. In instances where one individual seeks to assert dominance or exert control over the other, whether through vociferous outbursts or refusing

to engage and adopting a victim mentality, neither party is able to partake in a relationship that is characterized by maturity, equality, and affection.

First Day: The Profound Twelve

This particular journal exercise is anticipated to be the most arduous and time-consuming among all the exercises featured in this book, due to several factors. Initially, as you peruse the exercise, you will observe that there are several inquiries that require your attention, to be addressed in either succinct or extensive essay format, contingent upon your personal background. Furthermore, included at the conclusion of this chapter are a series of reflections on each question that I respectfully request you carefully peruse and contemplate upon as you evaluate your romantic history.

Ultimately, this particular section may elicit the most distressing experiences for individuals engaged in online dating, particularly those who have encountered painful romantic endings, endured instances of mistreatment, or grapple with internal personal conflicts that impede their dating prospects.

This book does not aim to provide remedies or curative solutions for the aforementioned circumstances. In the event that the exercise becomes excessively burdensome at any juncture, it is advisable to pause and resume only when and if you are capable. I strongly urge individuals who are finding this exercise problematic to contemplate seeking assistance from a certified medical or mental health practitioner.

Kindly respond to the subsequent inquiries to the fullest extent of your capability. Allow the answers to gracefully permeate your consciousness, and reflect upon the comprehensive scope of your romantic encounters.

What is the total number of enduring relationships, each lasting a minimum of one year, that you have been involved in? What were the reasons for the termination of these relationships?

How many brief interpersonal connections, characterized by a duration of less than one year, have you experienced? What were the reasons behind the termination of these relationships?

Which is more commonly observed: Do you tend to terminate relationships more frequently, or are you more often the recipient of relationship terminations?

Do you have a propensity for engaging in chaotic situations? Do you perceive yourself to flourish in more emotionally charged relationships?

Have you ever intentionally undermined or disrupted a relationship? Please provide a detailed account of any occurrences, if applicable, and the reasons that compelled you to terminate the courtship.

Could you please provide a comprehensive overview of your current physical, spiritual (if relevant), social, professional, and financial aspects of your life? Please ensure utmost honesty when answering this question, providing an accurate description of the state of your life in each of these areas. Is there anything you aspire to enhance in your abilities or skills? What aspects do you currently hold jurisdiction over? Do you perceive that these areas are hampering your progress in any capacity?

Do you have a tendency to hastily enter into one relationship after another, or are you an individual who exercises patience prior to embarking on a new relationship?

What are the most detrimental experiences you have encountered within your interpersonal connections? How did these events impact your sense of self and self-value? Have they had an impact on your self-esteem or exerted an influence on other relationships?

Do you identify as an introvert or an extrovert?

What factors do you believe ultimately restrict you from pursuing romantic relationships?

Do you harbor apprehension towards engaging in sexual activities or the potential hazards associated with sexually-transmitted infections (STIs)?
Are you of the opinion that your age renders you either too mature or too naïve to engage in romantic relationships?

After thoroughly and comprehensively addressing the aforementioned questions to the best of your abilities, proceed to read further and carefully contemplate the evaluation of your relationship as it is revealed by your responses.

Exploring the Depths of a Twelvefold Enigma

Prior to analyzing your responses and evaluating their implications for your requirements as an individual engaged in online dating, it is of utmost importance that you are aware of the following: your personal satisfaction holds paramount significance. For instance, following this exercise, it is possible that you may come to realize that a conventional marital arrangement does not align with your perception of an ideal relationship. Some individuals may encounter difficulty envisioning themselves engaging in numerous brief interpersonal connections. Irrespective of the discoveries made, it is crucial to refrain from succumbing to the temptation of drawing comparisons between oneself and another individual, or their respective experiences in the realm of dating. This is your world. Provided that you are at ease, feel free to explore it.

Inquiries numbered one and two
These inquiries aim to ascertain two patterns, specifically the average duration of your romantic partnerships. The second pattern entails discerning if there are any discernible patterns or trends concerning the reasons behind the termination of your relationships. Do you observe any resemblances? A particular student who underwent this

evaluation came to realize that the majority of her relationships were of a transient nature, ultimately culminating due to the fact that her partners primarily exploited her solely for sexual purposes. Furthermore, it was observed that another group of individuals saw the dissolution of their committed partnerships predominantly due to frequent disputes concerning financial matters. Attentively observe and record any recurring trends or patterns that can be discerned from your responses. These factors will warrant further exploration as we progress through our week-long expedition.

Questions No. 3-5
These three inquiries possess the potential to shed light on crucial aspects of your character and ascertain the adequacy of your past relationship matches. While reviewing your responses to these inquiries, please reflect on whether you have ever chosen to terminate a relationship due to a sense of ennui or tedium. Have your

previous romantic partnerships been characterized by disharmony and tumult? Do you find yourself drawn to individuals exhibiting rebellious traits or a rebellious nature of either gender? If you have deliberately undermined a relationship, was it motivated by an underlying and profound apprehension? Alternatively, have your interpersonal connections been tedious to such an extent that you felt an overwhelming desire to escape for the sake of preservation?

If any recurring themes have surfaced from these three inquiries, reflect upon the underlying factors that lead you to perceive them as pivotal elements in your romantic history. Record your answers.

Question No. 6
When an individual's life becomes imbalanced in any particular aspect, it has the potential to significantly compromise a relationship's prospects even before it has had a chance to flourish. If one finds oneself confronted

with health challenges, it has the potential to significantly dampen the experience of dating, if one permits it to do so. Nevertheless, embracing honesty and facing your circumstances truthfully will enable you to discover an ideal partner who possesses the capacity to support you in bearing that weight. Similarly, if the well-being of your spiritual state holds significance, it is imperative to seek a companion whose historical and personal convictions will reinforce those principles, enabling the both of you to progress collectively.

Have you ever been referred to as "overly dependent?" Your opportunities for social engagement may be severely limited. A well-rounded lifestyle ought to encompass both non-romantic and romantic interpersonal connections. It is imperative to have external support systems in place in order to maintain equilibrium. Furthermore, the adage holds true: the absence of a loved one indeed fosters even deeper affection. It is unreasonable to anticipate constant togetherness, excessive phone calls, or frequent texting, and still expect the relationship to endure.

Financial constraints can hinder individuals from pursuing romantic relationships as they may experience feelings of embarrassment stemming from their financial circumstances, including the inability to afford outings and limitations in transportation. Whilst it is incumbent upon us all to conduct ourselves diligently and fulfill our obligations, adversity can befall anyone without exception. Ultimately, your ideal partner will appreciate your inherent aspects as a human being, rather than evaluating your worth based on monetary possessions.

Question No. 7

Individuals who engage in a pattern of hastily transitioning from one relationship to another must exert effort in discerning the underlying reasons for their excessive need for companionship. Is it a result of the absence of one parent during childhood? Do you possess a fear of facing mortality without companionship? Take into meticulous consideration the underlying reasons for your inclination to pursue alternative distractions, instead of effectively addressing the emotional aftermath of your breakups. You may wish to consult a certified counselor or psychologist to explore effective coping mechanisms in the presence of these challenges.

Question No. 8
This inquiry seeks to establish the formation of negative mindsets and individual misconceptions. For certain participants, this evaluation demonstrates that their self-esteem has been influenced by verbal mistreatment endured in previous relationships, resulting in the attachment of specific derogatory terms to their identity. As an illustration, one student shares that he was informed by multiple former partners that he lacked physical attractiveness during the end of their relationships, which consequently impacted his self-perception and discernment of his worth. In addition, it

has been reported that she was subjected to persistent derogatory remarks about her weight by a former significant other, leading her to withdraw from romantic relationships due to a lack of self-esteem.

Disregard any negative experiences or mistreatment that may have been imposed upon you in the past. Your existence possesses inherent significance and worth. You are worthy of receiving love and I have faith in your eventual discovery of it. In the field of psychology, one may encounter the concept known as Maslow's Hierarchy of Needs, which posits that in order to sustain their existence, individuals require interpersonal respect, companionship, and fulfillment of their sexual needs, alongside other essential factors. Ultimately, we all possess the identical composition of bone, muscle, and tissue. Never let the negative experiences, challenging background, or malicious intentions of others impact your heart or mind under any circumstances. While I acknowledge the potential harm caused by their words and actions, I must emphasize that in order to attain your ideal partner, it is imperative that you release yourself from the burden of such experiences. I deeply apologize for the unfortunate occurrence that befell you, however, please be aware that the course of your life and the affection that awaits you cannot be influenced by the disparaging comments made by an embittered individual. You deserve good things.

Question No. 9
The outcome of this inquiry will have implications for subsequent activities during our week-long expedition, hence it is imperative to ensure their secure storage until we are able to revisit them.

Question No. 10
Please review the comments provided for Question No. 6.

Question No. 11
Sexually-transmitted infections (STIs) are undoubtedly a matter of significant

concern in contemporary society; nonetheless, it should not be a reason of sweeping magnitude to abstain from dating or engaging in physical intimacy. Frequently, our anxieties stem from our lack of knowledge. Acquire knowledge regarding sexually transmitted infections (STIs) and acquaint yourself with the necessary precautions to undertake when engaging in sexual activity. It is imperative to consistently prioritize the use of appropriate safeguards, ensuring a responsible approach towards sexual activity. Kindly reach out to your healthcare or mental health professionals to obtain guidance on finding secure avenues for physical self-expression.

Question No. 12
Love knows no expiration date. Several students have come to the realization that, upon attempting to answer this question, they have voluntarily isolated themselves due to a lack of perceived contributions. Meanwhile, it has come to the attention of others that their

challenges arise from having a preference for individuals who are either younger or older than themselves, thus restricting their potential connections. We shall delve deeper into these matters during our forthcoming expedition spanning seven days.

No Excuses

Criticism invariably inflicts emotional distress, and the forthcoming section is dedicated to the subject of criticism, or more significantly, the manner in which one may effectively address and react to critique. Chapter 1 may be somewhat challenging as it entails addressing all the detrimental thoughts that contribute to your unhappiness. It is imperative to expunge oneself of all emotional turmoil in order to progress and find closure.

Initially, let us endeavor to comprehend an anomalous aspect of human behavior. Numerous individuals who are discontentedly single nowadays actively or subconsciously make endeavors to evade encountering new individuals. Individuals, regardless of gender, have a propensity to verbally undermine their own state of contentment rather than directly confronting the distressing reality and embracing it. Yes, it's strange. Yes, it's sad. Additionally, you might indeed be culpable of engaging in the identical behavior.

To which uncomfortable truth am I referring? Censure! These are the entirety of the noxious ideas that we were deliberating upon. You are familiar with those particular ones. The inner dialogue that presents you with discouraging and unkind thoughts such as:

• You have exceeded the recommended weight for your height and body type.

• Your physique is quite slender.

• You possess an unattractive appearance. • Your physical characteristics are not visually appealing. • Your aesthetic qualities are lacking in attractiveness. • Your appearance is not regarded as attractive.

• You possess an excessive height.

• You possess a lack of height. • Your stature is insufficient. • You do not meet the desired standard of height. • Your vertical dimensions do not reach the normative expectations.

You have advanced in age." "Your age is exceeding the acceptable range." "You have surpassed the average age expectancy." "You've reached a stage of life that is considered more mature.

• You are of an age that is considered too young. • Your age does not meet the required threshold. • Based on your age, you do not meet the criteria. • It appears that you are underage for this particular situation.

• You are financially destitute. • Your financial situation is dire. • You have no funds. • You are in a state of financial insolvency.

• It appears that you have obtained a divorce. • It has come to my attention that you are now divorced. • A decree of divorce has been granted to you. • It seems that your marital status has changed and you are now legally divorced.

• Your appearance is unique and unconventional.

• You are excessively challenging!

How derogatory the language used is! Such expressions would likely be deemed unacceptable within a romantic relationship, and yet you might still find these thoughts directed towards oneself.

This behavior is highly detrimental to one's well-being and serves as a significant deterrent for individuals seeking fulfilling relationships. What is the point of exerting oneself when one is already aware of the inevitable outcome of failure? After careful consideration, it appears that you are inadequately worthy of a fulfilling relationship or, alternatively, he must meet a range of impractical criteria.

Instead of engaging in debates with these detrimental thoughts, a significant number of women opt to abstain from pursuing any opportunities. It is possible that they may prefer to await the arrival of an ideal individual who can rescue them from the harshness of reality. While it may be emotionally challenging to face criticism, it is imperative in order to disrupt the detrimental pattern of making justifications and evading one's desires.

Due to your apprehension towards encountering further negative ideas (frivolous criticisms that serve as reminders of your imperfections), it is plausible that you are rationalizing certain circumstances pertaining to your romantic relationships. Maybe you attempt to rationalize your way out of a promising relationship, holding the belief that your perceived shortcomings make it impossible for a man to ever love you, or that all the eligible individuals are already in committed partnerships.

Regardless of the justifications or negative thoughts that may be present, it is imperative that they come to an end today.

Removing the Road Blocks

Consider regarding negative thoughts and justifications (which are interconnected) as impediments hindering your ultimate path towards personal growth and success. To proceed along the path you seek, it is imperative to eliminate the impediment obstructing your way and subsequently forge ahead. If excuses and negative thought patterns act as hindrances, it is imperative for you to adopt resolute action in order to eliminate them from your psyche.

Proffering justifications and persuading oneself to forego novel opportunities is akin to halting and evading a nondescript container obstructing the pathway. The notion of allowing an unoccupied cardboard container to alter your intentions is undeniably humorous. Nevertheless, would you feel daunted if you were to encounter a complete row of cardboard boxes?

Alternatively, would you recollect that it is merely a vacuous container? Simply assert your presence and proceed forward while disregarding their presence. Is it feasible to eliminate the boxes as obstacles and continue progressing? Frequently, in the course of one's existence, the concept of the impediment proves to be considerably more formidable than the impediment itself.

A Critical Blow!
It is now appropriate to commence an experiment, and quite possibly one that may pose considerable challenges for you. I assure you that this will constitute the sole distressing aspect of this literary work. I am aware that it can be painful to face criticism, but engaging in this exercise is imperative if you desire to

bring about transformation in your life and achieve inner harmony. Ultimately, you will experience a greater sense of contentment upon successfully liberating yourself from the monotony of a routine and relinquishing the habit of making justifications.

I would appreciate it if you address and engage with the criticisms that have caused you distress. I kindly request that you eliminate from your thoughts any derogatory remarks you have made about yourself, and likewise discard any unfavorable judgements that others may have brought to your attention. Hold nothing back.

Rather than simply recalling a handful of phrases, consider contemplating the most unfavorable remarks that someone could conceivably make about you, directly addressing you." Now that you have harbored that distressing idea, I request you to articulate it audibly. Please endeavor to attempt it immediately.

It certainly causes discomfort, doesn't it? Nevertheless, I am pleased to inform you. Now that you have expressed and been informed of it, you have already encountered the most unfavorable outcome. You have already experienced that pivotal challenge and have emerged stronger as a result. At present, all surprises have been eliminated. Now, it is of no significance what opinions may be expressed by your acquaintances, relatives, or prospective partners. You have already conceived and articulated the most abhorrent ideas conceivable.

Given that these offensive remarks have been explicitly expressed, let them go. There is minimal benefit in constantly reiterating matters that are already known and have already been expressed. There no longer exists a threat of intimidation to deter you, nor any justification to evade listening to the repetition of your own statements by others.

Do not let criticism intimidate you. The sole aspect that genuinely causes distress in response to criticism is the identity of the individual expressing it. Is self-criticism not unattractive? You demonstrate self-care and self-sufficiency, yet you consistently belittle yourself in various situations. A lack of self-confidence can be a detrimental deterrent to one's motivation, resulting in the emergence of numerous challenges, ultimately deterring individuals from pursuing a straightforward path.

Chapter 1

Live your own life.

Engaging in a stimulating and fulfilling existence stands as the optimal means to enhance one's allure. Only those who exhibit manipulative tendencies or harbor insecurities are drawn to individuals devoid of hobbies, extracurricular pursuits, social connections, or passions. Take into account your personal inclinations:

Would you prefer to be in the company of an individual who dedicates his weekends to indulging in playing the cello, engaging in adventurous activities such as hiking and traveling, and escorting you to dance lessons? Alternatively, would you be more inclined to spend time with someone who predominantly prefers to lounge in the confines of their living space, engrossed in video games and television viewing? Allocate ample time for socializing with companions, cultivate personal hobbies, and undertake novel endeavors in order to uphold equivalent levels of personal accountability. (Indeed, in the event that you happen to encounter intriguing gentlemen during your visit!) Incorporate these facets of your exploration into your identity; refrain from forsaking them as soon as you encounter an individual. During this process, you will come to realize a heightened level of happiness and increased self-reliance, leading to more informed decisions in your dating endeavors and heightened compatibility with captivating individuals.

live your own life. The significance of each individual's life is as unique and personal as their own distinct fingerprint. In order to lead a fulfilling existence, it is imperative that you commence the process of discerning and assigning importance to the elements in your life that hold the utmost significance to you. It is imperative that you engage in a rigorous assessment to determine if you are genuinely leading the desired life. Do your life choices exemplify your aspirations, beliefs, and moral principles? Alternatively, do you adhere to the expectations set by individuals in your inner circle and the principles instilled in you through past teachings? To express the concept differently, whose existence are you guiding?

Discovering your unique path may require a considerable amount of time and persistent experimentation. The process of uncovering one's true identity is a lifelong endeavor. Our personalities, interests, and aptitudes may undergo transformations as time progresses. As individuals capable of adaptation, we possess the ability to undergo changes at any given moment. Prior to seeking personal or life enhancements, it is essential to gain a comprehensive understanding of our own identity.

Five Steps to Achieve Autonomy and Lead a Fulfilling Life.

1. Take into account your authentic aspirations and desires in life.
Comprehending our desires in life may pose a challenge for a significant number of individuals. However, without explicit identification of those parameters, it becomes implausible to lead a life in accordance with one's own prerogatives. Understanding your desires and discerning their significance can assist you in establishing priorities, formulating goals, and ultimately attaining your desired outcome. When

one possesses a clear understanding of their desires, they possess a specific destination and can methodically plan a path towards it. In the words of Dr. Lisa Firestone, "If one lacks clarity on their desires, they resemble a vessel adrift without the guidance of a rudder."

Engaging in introspection by posing the following inquiries can facilitate the discovery of your innermost desires. What holds utmost significance in my life? Rather than becoming preoccupied with your perceived obligations or others' expectations, grant yourself the freedom to engage in independent thinking while reflecting upon these inquiries.

It is a common misconception that contemplating our desires is an act of self-centeredness; however, this introspective process plays an essential role in self-discovery. It is not essential to neglect the principles of others in order to reflect upon your own. However, determining your priorities involves recognizing the individuals who hold significance in your life, acknowledging their value in your existence, and understanding that taking care of them is a substantial aspect of your happiness and the meaningfulness of your life. Moreover, as Dr. Lisa Firestone asserts, your exceptional talents, once identified and cultivated, hold immense significance within your immediate environment and beyond.

While it may appear trite to offer counsel such as "pursue your passion," substantial evidence indicates that adhering to this principle not only engenders personal contentment but also enhances the likelihood of attaining success in one's chosen professional endeavors and recreational pursuits. Based on a recent empirical investigation into the effects of motivation, it was revealed that individuals demonstrated a higher likelihood of achievement when their drive originated from internal factors as opposed to external incentivization.

Therefore, contemplate the aspects that hold significance to you.

2. Distinguish Yourself.
Each one of us possesses inherent genetic uniqueness from the moment of our birth. Nevertheless, the early contexts in which we are nurtured play a significant role in shaping our individuality; rather than developing our own distinct personas, we often internalize the qualities of those who care for us. As a result, we often allocate a greater amount of time to experiencing and participating in the lives of others, relatively neglecting our own existence. According to Dr. Robert Firestone's publication entitled The Self-Under Siege: A Therapeutic Model for Differentiation, it is imperative for individuals to disengage from adverse environmental factors in order to lead autonomous lives and fulfill their innate potential."

As per the insights of Dr. Robert Firestone, interactions between individuals that either hinder or facilitate the personal growth and formation of one's character over the course of their lifetime bear influence on the individual's authentic sense of self. We develop adaptive strategies as we progress to address feelings of discomfort and anxiety. We adapt to conform to our initial environment and fulfill our desires. One approach we employ involves acquiring negative attributes from our parents' or caregivers' personalities, or creating psychological barriers in response to such traits. In order to lead autonomous lives and accomplish our individual aspirations, it is imperative for us to distance ourselves from detrimental familial and cultural influences.

Confronted with the challenge of self-identity, a majority of individuals find themselves either conforming to the value systems and belief frameworks instilled by their families and societies, or conversely, engaging in rebellion by adopting oppositional perspectives that directly contradict those of their familial and cultural backgrounds. Rather than simply accepting or rejecting the values and ideas imparted by your early influences, it is imperative to proactively establish your individual values and beliefs in order to lead a self-determined life. Consequently, in order to bestow your life with a heightened sense of meaning, it is advisable to strive towards embodying your principles.

We have the potential to define our own identities by distancing ourselves from the detrimental influences and associations of our previous experiences. To the extent that we can discern, cultivate our individual identities, and pursue our distinct aspirations, we shall attain the highest level of fulfillment in our lives. Rather than adhering to the regulations established by our parents, family, or society, it is imperative that we strive to lead an autonomous existence.

3. Set objectives.

Establishing personal goals becomes imperative once an individual has identified their aspirations and core values. What actions are necessary in order to lead a self-directed existence? It is advantageous to document your objectives. Rather than burdening yourself with an extensive inventory of modifications you wish to make, commence with just a handful. Please contemplate the specific measures you can undertake in order to achieve your goals. Establish attainable objectives in the initial stages and progressively advance towards them. It would be advisable for you to take personal accountability and closely track your advancements by utilizing these waypoints. In the event that your intention is to compose and publish a novel, your primary aim could be to finalize one chapter within the following fourteen days.

Based on a recent research, the act of documenting goals, formulating a strategic course of action, and providing weekly updates to an accountability partner significantly enhanced the probability of individuals achieving their desired outcomes. You may consider employing that approach in order to achieve your objectives. Do you happen to have an acquaintance who might be able to provide assistance and hold you accountable for the attainment of your goals? Request assistance from them.

The establishment and fulfillment of goals is an indispensa Rather than proactively undertaking the requisite actions to fulfill our goals, a significant portion of our collective tends to engross themselves in idle fantasies regarding those objectives. According to the words of Nolan Bushnell, it is a universally observed phenomenon that every individual who has engaged in the act of bathing has experienced moments of inspiration. The actions are not always straightforward and often push us beyond our boundaries of comfort, yet there are no shortcuts to leading a purposeful existence. It is incumbent upon individuals to step out of the shower, towel themselves dry, and take proactive measures. If living life is your intention, it is imperative that you proactively seize opportunities and shape your own path.

4. Ceasing the influence of your internal critic.
Exercise mindfulness towards the impediments that may impede your progress as you embark on the path towards your aspirations. The initial adversary you will encounter is your "critical inner voice," which can be likened to an unfavorable coach residing within our minds. It encompasses detrimental ideologies, perspectives, and conducts that erode our sense of value and contradict our optimal welfare. It poses as our most formidable foe.

This internal voice meticulously examines each of our actions, belittles us, and instills uncertainty in our aspirations through remarks such as, "You lack desire, don't you?"

You are unlikely to achieve success, thus making it futile to pursue such an endeavor. It advises us against the pursuit of our desires. By upholding your defensive coping mechanisms and clinging to the familiar persona you constructed during childhood, the inner critic endeavors to maintain a sense of security within you. Your inner critic will provide a multitude of justifications for why you are unable or should abstain from leading your own life. It is imperative that you detach yourself from your internal evaluator and cease heeding its imprudent counsel. Identify the origin of this self-critical inner voice. It might be advantageous to perceive this critical internal voice as the expression of the anti-self, or that facet of one's being that opposes personal well-being. Everyone is split. Our authentic identities, characterized by compassion towards both ourselves and others, are in conflict with our contrary identities, marked by self-loathing, distrust towards others, and in extreme cases, self-destructive tendencies and the mistreatment of others. Our authentic identities are shaped by our specific passions and desires. It possesses goals and upholds the principle of existence. The intensity of these internal 'voices' could potentially increase as you consciously distance yourself from the critical self-talk and begin prioritizing your personal needs, desires, and goals. When individuals embark on the pursuit of their goals, they often experience heightened levels of concern as an outcome. Your internal censor will often endeavor to undermine your endeavors by instilling self-doubt in your thoughts or enticing you towards procrastination.

If you are genuinely committed to enhancing your life, it is imperative to adopt an unwavering stance against your internal critic. Once you attain the consciousness that you are engaging in self-criticism, promptly cease such negative ideation. Do not expend valuable time in the pursuit of uncovering the core veracity within your internal critic's severe evaluation, whilst you appraise its flawed guidance. Refrain from succumbing to the notion that these thoughts are valid, but rather recognize them as negative internal reflections. It is important to acknowledge that nurturing such acerbic self-perceptions is not suitable or conducive to personal growth. Please take heed of the factors that contribute to your negative thinking. Please be mindful that your "perceptions" have a cunning ability to discern possible truths. Your internal censor will often direct its attention towards your imperfections. Take caution of notions such as 'there is no need to exercise today,' which may appear agreeable or tempting but can have adverse effects on your objectives or ultimate welfare. Do not allow yourself to be misled by the murmurings within your mind, for they are devoid of genuine concern for your well-being. You deserve a break.

5. Utilize Your Power.

Your level of confidence will increase as you overcome the voice of self-doubt within you. In order to lead an autonomous existence, one must harness their own capabilities. It represents a constructive manifestation of self-affirmation that embodies an inherent pursuit of affection, accomplishment, contentment, and purpose within an individual's existence. According to Dr. Robert Firestone, the concept of "personal power" encompasses attributes such as resilience, self-assurance, and proficiency that individuals gradually cultivate during their personal growth and maturation. Progressing towards the actualization of one's true potential and aspiring to achieve greater goals in life is indicative of inner strength, symbolizing the authentic essence of an individual.

As per the insights from Dr. Firestone, personal power can be defined as "an attitude or state of mind." Consequently, it is possible for us to foster and develop this attribute. We cultivate our resilience through internalizing self-criticism, establishing a profound connection with our unique interests, and actively striving towards our goals.

Experiencing life on one's own entails neither an augmented level of challenge nor an escalated level of gratification. Do not fear death, but rather lament the unfulfilled potential of the life that remains unexplored, as aptly expressed by Natalie Babbitt. There is no obligation for you to exist indefinitely. It is imperative that you solely focus on enduring and persevering.

Dating a Banker
Typically, certain individuals are disinclined to engage in romantic relationships with bankers due to perceiving them as excessively occupied and single-minded in their pursuits. However, if your preference lies solely in pursuing a romantic connection with an individual who possesses refined skills

in wining and dining, then opting for a banker would be most suitable. They are impeccably groomed, articulate, and possess a high level of academic attainment. Bankers offer delightful indulgences, showcasing the utmost regal treatment for their esteemed clientele. While in the company of a banker, there is no need to concern yourself with reaching for your wallet, yet it is prudent to be cautious, as a certain level of hubris is an inherent trait among them.

It is inequitable to make sweeping generalizations about the attractive qualities commonly displayed by bankers, as individuals of virtues and vices can be found across all societal spheres. Still, they are workaholic. If it does not pertain to a scheduled meeting with a prospective client, my time will be allocated to the completion of an excel spreadsheet.

If one wishes to engage in a romantic relationship with individuals working in the banking field, it is imperative to be aware of certain aspects regarding their profession.

1. Dedicated individuals with a strong work ethic

Numerous financial professionals dedicate significant hours to their work. This implies that they operate continuously, without interruption, even during weekends. Indeed, they demonstrate unwavering dedication to their work, exhibiting exceptional focus which leaves limited opportunity for leisure activities. Consequently, bankers do not require individuals who cause them distress. They are unable to endure the persistence of a significant other as they typically experience sufficient stress in their daily work routine.

2. Bankers possess extensive intelligence and knowledge

Bankers demonstrate discerning intellect and exhibit a preparedness for cognitive aptitude. Typically, they adhere to the standards depending on the nature of your interaction with them. However, the true test lies in whether they adhere to a set of misguided principles as revealed by the unfolding of time.

3. They consistently maintain a high level of organization.

In adherence to their workplace ethical standards, they value organizational structure. Due to their intense dedication to their profession, it is likely that bankers may not be inclined to socialize during regular days. However, despite this, they continue to spend time with you on Saturdays. You are able to harness their full potential.

Bankers, conversely, will aspire to possess gates that will harmonize with their professional endeavors.

4. Individual with a caring demeanor

Due to the inherent demands of their occupation, they are unable to allocate time for the maintenance of their residences. They are willing to cover the costs of all domestic services. Despite being in the comfort of their own home, they exhibit signs of fatigue. Following a day immersed in their field of work, they require individuals who will provide them with guidance and support, while absolutely avoiding any association with toxic individuals.

5. Engage in the exchange of ideas Discuss and exchange thoughts and perspectives Contribute to the sharing of ideas Participate in the dissemination of ideas

There are numerous strategies available to effectively cope with stress, such as engaging in social activities with individuals who share common interests. This allows for a mutual exchange of thoughts, ideas, aspirations, and objectives once you return to your residence. Consider the prospect of having a partner of comparable success who actively supports and contributes to the attainment of your shared aspirations and life goals.

Dating a Divorcee

Engaging in romantic relationships post-divorce can be quite intricate and challenging, typically proving to be a formidable endeavor for those involved. This is due to the considerable pain and emotional strain that arises from the termination of a long-term romantic relationship, rendering the process of rebuilding and moving on exceedingly challenging. In order to attain true happiness and progress forward, it is imperative that one conscientiously relinquishes and dismisses any lingering recollections and emotions pertaining to one's estranged partner. You may still harbor unresolved matters stemming from your prior dating or marital experience that could potentially impact your burgeoning relationship. Make every effort to resolve these issues prior to resuming your romantic relationship.

Prior to embarking on this second missionary voyage, it would be prudent to establish a set of foundational guidelines. It is imperative to ascertain your intentions before embarking on a date, determining whether you seek a committed partner or are simply engaging in casual dating for amusement. It is essential to be forthright and truthful about your motives. Strive for honesty and refrain from falsehoods. Integrity must remain your guiding principle and foremost value in the realm of resuming your dating life.

Please find presented herein a collection of factors worthy of contemplation prior to reentering the realm of dating.

Self-confidence

It is imperative to have faith in oneself on this occasion. Do not develop premature emotional attachments to individuals during initial encounters and remain authentic to your true self. In the event that the date does not yield the desired outcome, it is imperative to possess the self-assurance necessary to persevere, making successive attempts until success is achieved. May you not find the concept of rejection burdensome. Displaying a sense of assurance and refraining from dwelling on negative thoughts during your rendezvous will greatly contribute to your long-term success.

Wise choice

Exercise caution when deciding upon an alternative date. There exists a general principle which suggests refraining from pursuing a romantic relationship with an individual who had previous involvement with you during the course of your divorce. Although you may perceive this individual as an ideal match for yourself, it is common for individuals with such perceptions to ultimately compromise and settle for a marriage that may not be entirely satisfactory. Consequently, you may find yourself entangled in another complicated situation, despite the existence of extraordinary circumstances. Should you wish to pursue romantic involvement once more, I advise you to be deliberate in your decision-making and exercise discernment.

Be gentle with yourself

A divorced individual requires a significant period of relaxation to recover from the initial experience of a missionary endeavor. It is imperative that they allocate sufficient time and personal space to gradually reintegrate themselves into the situation at hand. Act in a callous and composed manner during the initial stages of your romantic encounters. Indeed, it is advantageous to present oneself in an elegant manner and display one's utmost appearance; there is nothing objectionable about it.

Looking good and wearing a cute outfit is part of the practice and ways to regain self-confidence. Appear elegant and exude an impeccable aura while engaging in such endeavors.

Refrain from engaging in romantic activities during evening hours.

It is advisable to refrain from engaging in nighttime dating, such as on popular evenings like Saturday and Friday nights, as a starting point. In the interim, individuals who have undergone divorce should consider scheduling their dates on weekdays, including Monday through Thursday, as well as on Sunday evenings. Evening rendezvous will engender and nurture a romantic and endearing ambiance. Therefore, opt for evening appointments during the initial stages of dating.

When children are involved

Individuals interested in pursuing a romantic relationship with a person who has gone through a divorce should take into account the welfare and well-being of the children involved. Furthermore, it should be acknowledged that becoming a parent does not necessitate the cessation of post-divorce dating. In fact, it is entirely feasible for one's new partner to actively involve and engage with one's children, enhancing the enjoyment of the relationship. The dissolution of a marriage should ideally bring about as much joy to the children involved. Nevertheless, the task of seeking a romantic partner becomes notably less complex in the absence of parental responsibilities since one's focus and time will not be divided.

Refrain from discussing your previous romantic partner.

Having reached the decision to pursue romantic relationships following your divorce, it is imperative that you refrain from discussing your former spouse. Discussing a former partner typically occurs when one continues to harbor the emotional connection experienced during the prior relationship. Engaging in the practice of comparing your current companion to your former partner will result in significant consequences. Hence, endeavor to steer clear of it.

Identify Shared Interests And Attributes

Hence, you exhibited self-restraint by refraining from contacting him for a duration of several days. Over the course of the preceding days, he has pondered the nature of your being. If he had shown interest in you, it is likely that he had been thinking about you frequently during these past few days. One notable characteristic of males is their tendency to refrain from initiating contact following a meeting, as they harbor concerns regarding the possibility of conveying inaccurate messages. At present, he remains uncertain of whether you have disregarded his invitation or if you intend to reconnect with him. One advantage of postponing for a few days is that it currently places him at a slight disadvantage. The individual is uncertain as to whether they should adopt an assertive or non-confrontational stance, which aligns precisely with your preferences. He is unaware, to his detriment, that you hold complete sway over your destiny, and the forthcoming dates will provide a more definitive impression of whether he is deserving of your companionship.

Kindly send him a concise message to inquire whether he would be interested in arranging a meeting at the nearby café for a beverage. Please be aware that this gathering is solely a meeting, and there is no need for apprehension or confusion regarding any romantic implications resembling a date. When one becomes excessively engrossed in the realm of romantic pursuits, errors tend to occur and a tendency to adopt an inauthentic persona may arise. It is premature at this stage to convey any indications regarding your intentions to him. By convening for a casual coffee gathering, you alleviate the burden and strain placed upon yourself. When convening at the coffee shop, please conduct yourself as if you are meeting a familiar acquaintance, casually dropping by for a brief beverage and enjoyable dialogue. This visit will be of brief duration, with the primary objective being to acquaint ourselves with his personality and determine any shared interests between the two of you. It is important to comprehend that shared interests or traits are not requisite for a successful interpersonal relationship. Numerous couples derive pleasure from their differences as it contributes to the rejuvenation of their relationship. Please refrain from approaching this meeting with the sole purpose of seeking commonalities with him. It is important to recognize that this meeting is intended for casual conversation only.

Whilst discussing the matter of profession, endeavor to ascertain whether he possesses a particularized vocation or if he is engaged in a novel occupation. Recall the previous encounter wherein he made reference to the baseball game. Attempt to engage in a meaningful discussion in order to ascertain his interests in sports, cinema, or outdoor activities. Inquiry into a gentleman's recreational activities may occasionally be construed in a negative manner. This is an inappropriate time for engaging in sexual innuendo, hence I suggest seeking answers to your inquiries by observing the topics he discusses. It can be inferred that he thoroughly enjoys engaging in sports activities during his leisure hours, given his constant discussion about the subject matter. Identifying shared attributes is crucial to ascertaining his compatibility as a prospective long-term partner. If you have a strong inclination towards cycling or running, and he expresses a genuine fondness for mountain hiking, it is reasonable to assume that the two of you can effectively explore an abundance of outdoor activities together.

Merely because he expresses his enthusiasm for tinkering with his car during his leisure hours does not warrant your dismissal of him as a mechanic consumed by his passion, leaving no room for enjoyable shared activities with you. Cease such contemplation immediately, lest you jeopardize the safety and integrity of the vessel whilst it resides at the dock. To establish a strong basis, it suffices to discover a few minor points of convergence with him. It is highly likely that he is somewhat perplexed as to why you took several days to send him a text message. The majority of gentlemen are unaccustomed to the extended period of time it takes for a young lady to initiate contact via text. This meeting presents a singular occasion to gauge the individual, and should you discern certain aspects of the discussion that suggest he is the ideal candidate, then it is prudent to proceed expeditiously. By discerning a shared attribute, it becomes evident that the prospect of cultivating a connection is feasible. However, to accomplish this, it is imperative to proceed with caution and exhibit the commendable quality of authenticity. You have not erred thus far, as his knowledge about you is limited. However, the information he possesses about you hitherto is entirely accurate. Inform him that you thoroughly enjoyed his company, but unfortunately, you must promptly depart. However, you assure him that you will make it a point to communicate with him via text or phone within a few days. That will assuredly be an unforeseen development for him. Based on two preceding encounters, he conjectures that you likely possess an interest. Let us proceed to the subsequent chapter, wherein you shall soon discover how the presence of insecurity can swiftly cause the loss of the individual concerned.

Striving To Find The Ideal Life Partner

Do you hold the belief that soul mates exist? If you are currently seeking your soulmate and have not yet found them, do not despair. This all-encompassing guide on discovering your life partner may prove invaluable in locating your distinct match.

The pursuit of romantic relationships can be challenging on certain occasions; there is no doubt about it. It can be disheartening to engage in a succession of dates or pursue relationships with the hope of finding your perfect match, only to realize that the person in question is simply incompatible with you. Investing one's time in a relationship that is destined for failure is a futile endeavor. However, conversely, after a period of solitude, it becomes exceedingly challenging.

We dedicate a considerable amount of time searching for a suitable life partner who can bring happiness and affection into our lives. Occasionally, we are fortunate enough to encounter the person we are destined to spend our lives with during our initial sincere encounter. In various circumstances, it may necessitate additional effort and investigation. However, the truth of the matter is that there exists an ideal partner destined for each and every one of us.

There is a high likelihood that they are in close proximity and actively pursuing love as well. And it is imperative that you fully comprehend this fact: the task of uncovering the methods to encounter your soulmate is not as arduous as it is often depicted.

It is not as arduous as the task of finding a needle in a haystack. In fact, it is as effortless as a leisurely walk in the park. Ideally, a brief walk would suffice.

What is a soulmate?
Soulmates are a topic of widespread discussion, yet it seems that few truly comprehend its significance in

contemporary times. You may be in pursuit of one, however, are you acquainted with the authentic traditional notion of a soulmate? There exist two potential interpretations, yet their veracity remains indeterminable to the living.

1. The two ethereal beings united as a singular entity.

In accordance with a particular delineation, a dyadic arrangement of ethereal entities is partitioned within the realm of spirituality, thereby manifesting in two separate corporeal vessels. Both of these individuals spend their entire lives in search of their life partners and do not find solace until they encounter each other and develop mutual affection, consequently reuniting.

2. A singular entity divided into two beings.

Now, according to an alternative legendary belief, it is postulated that a single soul undergoes division, giving rise to two distinct entities which manifest themselves in the form of two human bodies existing on the terrestrial plane. Neither of these components can attain contentment or affection until they reunite into a singular entity once more.

The legitimacy of these criteria remains uncertain as it is unclear whether they are genuinely established or mere fabrications intended to enhance the perceived value of a romantic relationship. However, it remains a commendable idea.

The precise elucidation of a soulmate,

Do we subscribe to the notion of soulmates? Indeed, we do! However, there is some pertinent information that you should be aware of. One may diligently quest both near and far in pursuit of that perfect companion, but it is imperative to grasp this undeniable truth if one wishes to acquaint themselves with the methods for finding their soulmate.

In our perspective, we propose the authentic characterization of a soulmate: Soulmates do not come into existence by birth; rather, they are forged through interconnectedness. Soulmates are formed through the cultivation of love and compromise, and they are molded by two profound affections that possess a profound understanding, mutual respect, and genuine admiration for each other.

If you perceive a consistent deepening of affection for one another as time progresses, and if either of you endeavors to provide solace and nurture towards the other in earnest, you are well on the path towards attaining a spiritual connection as soulmates.

Ultimately, two individuals who are fundamentally incompatible can never transcend their differences and form a deep connection as soulmates. It encompasses aspects beyond mere affection and longing; it requires unwavering devotion and the willingness to selflessly cater to each other's happiness to truly establish a profound soulmate connection.

The appropriate methodology for locating your companion

It is not advisable to accept a partner who is not entirely suitable, or relinquish your pursuit of finding a compatible life partner. Nevertheless, it seems that your quest may be eternal. What would be the potential scenario if your destined partner is an individual whom you have yet to encounter in person? Does a solitary life await?

It is imperative that we refrain from entering into relationships with individuals whom we recognize as unsuitable for us, individuals who demonstrate unfair treatment towards us, or individuals who do not align with us in terms of compatibility. Friendship is accessible to individuals of all backgrounds. Therefore, I encourage you to continue your diligent search and maintain a positive outlook.

36 Genuine Methods to Discover Your Perfect Life Partner
What specific criteria must be met for an individual to be deemed your genuine romantic partner? May I inquire as to

their whereabouts? Presented below are the comprehensive procedures that encompass every necessary aspect for swiftly identifying your ideal soulmate.

One could choose to patiently await the advent of love, however, there is the potential for it to never come to fruition. At times, embarking on a voyage is necessary to encounter that unique individual capable of captivating one's senses.

To unveil the secret of uncovering your soulmate, embark upon a journey of daring romantic endeavors. The more promptly you embark on the endeavor to encounter that elusive counterpart, the more expeditiously you shall discover your chivalrous suitor or fair maiden.

Are you experiencing uncertainty regarding the path ahead? Contained herein are all the areas in which you have the ability to make modifications, and rest assured, your compatible life partner will manifest itself expeditiously. Additionally, the journey of discovering true love would indeed be an extraordinary and unforgettable expedition.

Adhere to these guidelines, and you will progressively draw nearer to your partner with each successive day.

1. Aim to attain the highest version of yourself.

Peruse the mirror. What do you perceive, do you deem acceptable? In order to discover your ideal companion, it is imperative that you endeavor to achieve a state of flawlessness as well. Each of us adorns fashionable shaded eyewear, causing our initial perception to be superficial. When one exudes self-assurance regarding their appearance and manner of self-expression in the presence of potential life partners, it becomes comparatively simpler to capture their notice.

Inside your physical being lies an ideal version of yourself, eagerly poised for transformation. Unveil that striking individual, and you will witness a significant boost in your self-confidence. Furthermore, it is apparent when you exude a sense of poise and self-assurance in your overall demeanor and presentation.

2. One must possess unwavering belief in one's abilities.
Prioritize internal reconciliation prior to seeking a life partner. Your soulmate's ability to establish a genuine connection with you may be hindered if you engage in a new relationship characterized by feelings of anxiety or self-loathing.

3. Have clear goals.
Ensure that you possess a clear understanding of the attributes you desire in a prospective companion. What is of utmost importance to you? What brings you joy? Moreover, having an understanding of one's preferences enables easier differentiation between a potentially promising relationship and an unfavorable one.

4. Acknowledge and identify the origins of your personal feelings of fondness.

Subsequent to the identification of one's romantic partner, experiencing feelings of affection should inherently occur. It is important to be attentive to the factors that evoke feelings of love within you, enabling you to identify them as they gradually manifest themselves.

5. Remain cognizant of your life's goals.
It is of utmost importance to establish a shared vision for the future. Seek out individuals who align with your aspirations and vision for your life, especially if you are cognizant of your objectives and the necessary steps to realize them.

6. Understand your values.
Each individual possesses distinct values and beliefs, alongside those that they find morally abhorrent. Display forthrightness and sincerity in expressing your convictions. Identify an individual who upholds and abides by these principles.

7. Squeeze some frogs.

Life does not mirror the realm of cinema, and in stark contrast to the filming process, the opportunity for redemption eludes you when you find yourself entwined with a person who does not truly align with your soul.

Nevertheless, it does not constitute a negative aspect. Determining your authentic requirements in a prospective partner necessitates a process of experimentation, evaluation, courtship, and developing deep affection. Anticipate encountering several disappointments before encountering the one who will truly capture your heart.

Each and every new encounter, casual or committed, will impart valuable insights regarding matters of love, self-discovery, and the attributes and aspirations one seeks in a significant other. However, it is solely through embracing romantic risks that you can acquire such invaluable lessons.

8. Follow your heart

Do you have an affinity for culinary arts, expressing oneself through rhythmic movement, or embarking on exhilarating expeditions up majestic peaks? To acquire knowledge of discovering love, it is essential to actively pursue and engage in activities that bring fulfillment and purpose to your life. When engaging in communal activities, you will undoubtedly encounter numerous individuals who fervently share your passion. If by chance you happen to come across someone whom you find appealing while actively pursuing your interests, it will bring you one step closer to connecting with your ideal counterpart.

9. Pursue novel endeavors

Do you encounter challenges when it comes to finding individuals who captivate your interest? Have you thoroughly searched all the appropriate locations? Do you possess the capacity to perceive beyond the confines of your limited realm of existence?

A significant portion of individuals within our community prefer the familiarity and security of their insular reality. We do not derive pleasure from exploring novel experiences or acquainting ourselves with unfamiliar individuals. However, it is imperative that you venture into the realm of unfamiliar experiences in order to genuinely discover your ideal life partner. Please do not decline the invitation extended by your friends to participate in either a whitewater rafting or hill climbing expedition. Experiment with novel experiences, explore various possibilities, and embrace the abundance of life. More often than not, in the most unforeseen circumstances, one tends to encounter their life partner while embarking on a novel expedition.

An advantageous aspect is that one does not necessarily need to put their life on hold in search of love. Alternatively, you may choose to embrace life in its entirety. Unforeseen by even the most astute, existence possesses a remarkable inclination to bestow upon you delightful unexpected occurrences.

Cease Forming Opinions Based On Movies Or Books.

I apologize for potentially deflating any idealized notions, but it is essential to acknowledge that genuine love does not consistently encompass the same magnitude of emotions depicted when a wealthy individual falls for someone of lower socioeconomic status, as illustrated in films or literature. The central characters in fictional narratives tend to possess more elevated social status than those encountered in reality. Consequently, it is imperative to refrain from establishing impracticable benchmarks.

8. Refrain from placing emphasis on your physical appearance.

Unconditional love epitomizes a love that is devoid of any conditions or expectations. It signifies that one's affections are not contingent upon another person's physical attractiveness.

While a pleasing appearance may be viewed as an added advantage, it is not a prerequisite. Instead, the focus should be on finding a life companion with whom one can cultivate a harmonious and contented existence. The foremost considerations should revolve around shared values, admirable character traits, and compatible personalities.

9. Seek out an individual whose personality aligns harmoniously with your own.

The presence of "irreconcilable differences" between partners, stemming from incongruous personalities, could lead to the termination of a relationship. Consequently, it is advisable to seek a future partner whose personality harmonizes with one's own, thereby cultivating a sense of balance in the union.

The deficiencies of one partner should be compensated for by the strengths of the other. Consider, for example, a hypothetical couple who possess ingenious business ideas but lack the determination to bring them to fruition. In this scenario, their partner should possess the resilience and aptitude required to transform those ideas into viable commercial enterprises.

CHAPTER 4

10. SEEK OUT AN INDIVIDUAL WHOSE PRIORITIES COINCIDE WITH YOUR OWN.

The alignment of priorities can significantly impact a relationship, not just personality traits. Disagreements regarding what takes precedence can pose substantial challenges. For example, if a husband prioritizes family obligations above all else, while his wife is more career-oriented, they may grapple with a lack of mutual understanding.

11. Seek out an individual who holds you in high regard.

An individual's capacity to elicit smiles and convey affection may not suffice. Seek out someone who comprehends the importance of treating others with respect, irrespective of their age, status, or relationship. Why is this paramount? The propensity for selflessness is more probable in individuals who possess sensitivity towards the rights and emotions of others. This attribute indicates their conscientiousness in avoiding any harm towards you, thereby fostering a sense of safety in their presence.

Consider the potential perceptions and evaluations of your friends and family.

It is advisable to acquaint the individual with your family and acquaintances prior to commencing a romantic union. When enamored, one can become infatuated and thus lose objectivity. Consequently, it is prudent to solicit the perspectives of those who are intimately connected to you.

It is imperative that you make inquiries regarding the reasons behind your friends and family's disapproval of the individual whom you hold affection for. Endeavor to adopt their perspective in order to assess whether or not you remain inclined to pursue the burgeoning relationship.

CHAPTER 5

CHAPTER 5

13. DEVELOP FAMILIARITY WITH THEIR FRIENDS AND FAMILY MEMBERS.

If one encounters an individual within their customary milieu, it offers an enhanced opportunity for understanding their true essence. This scenario encompasses their interactions with beloved companions and relatives. By engaging with their social circle, one can witness firsthand their conduct towards oneself and vice versa.

If an individual establishes an affectionate and harmonious bond with their loved ones, they are likely to excel in their behavior towards them. In case the relationship appears to be lacking warmth and intimacy, it is advisable to assess alternative courses of action.

Please allow for a sufficient amount of time for the solution to take effect.

Time is often regarded as the ultimate litmus test of love. It is not uncommon for couples to experience the tarnishing of their affectionate bond with the advent of disagreements, which tend to arise after the initial phase of attraction, a period that typically spans a year. This phenomenon is attributed to a decrease in enthusiasm and an increase in disparities. This predicament has the potential to endure for a duration of up to three years.

Due to the extensive duration of your acquaintance and companionship, the relationship might potentially descend into tedium and monotony in the forthcoming years. Consequently, numerous individuals are enticed to seek out new connections. However, if your relationship endures and prospers, it is a testament to the authenticity of your affection.

15. Avoid allowing your emotions to influence your decision-making.

Enamoration often clouds rationality, as I previously indicated. It is important to recognize that authentic love surpasses mere sentiments. Exercise caution before embracing someone into your life hastily; several underlying factors must contribute to your ultimate determination. Reference the earlier counsel to ascertain if the individual aligns with the criteria for genuine love.

CHAPTER TWO

Locations Where You Can Encounter Your Ideal Life Partner

Upon reflection, encountering an individual while in flight seems rather enchanting. There exist various splendid and unforeseen avenues through which one may come across their destined companion, hence it is advised not to disregard the ensuing suggestions:

The gym is unrivaled in terms of its excellence.

If you share a similar experience as me, you emerge from each exercise session appearing moist and sweaty. The gym is not appropriate for expressing your outward attractiveness, however, if you are truly devoted to someone, constant elegance is not necessary. When you feel prepared, make your approach to establish familiarity with a frequent visitor at the gym. If approaching strangers makes you nervous, request a friend to join you to avoid sounding like a schoolgirl. You are definitely not the sole individual in possession of this plate.

Your residential development or community

Engaging in romantic relationships with your roommates is generally ill-advised, while pursuing a romantic connection with someone residing in your immediate vicinity presents less significant concerns. If you are a resident of a vast residential complex, a communal gathering hosted within the building may serve as the opportune occasion to encounter a potential romantic partner, or at the very least, establish amiable relationships with fellow residents. Following the completion of one's college education, it becomes increasingly challenging to establish connections with unfamiliar individuals. Therefore, it is advisable not to exhibit reluctance in initiating interactions with individuals residing in your vicinity or occupying the same building while they are engaging in various activities.

On a flight

Please refrain from repeating the error I committed by avoiding the opportunity to engage with a potential individual of gentlemanly or captivating nature during your future encounters on a Boeing 737.

In the workplace

Office romances have the potential to be highly detrimental, as the consequences can extend beyond the workplace. However, it is important to acknowledge that such relationships may also lead to lasting friendships. It is not surprising that the office and school are widely regarded as prime locations to encounter potential acquaintances or romantic partners. If individuals are employed within the same professional domain, it is highly probable that they possess comparable interests and possess an understanding of one another's operational procedures.

If individuals are employed within the same professional domain, it is highly probable that they possess comparable interests and possess an inherent comprehension towards one another's operational processes.

If you are employed within the same professional domain, it is highly probable that you would possess comparable interests and possess an intricate comprehension of one another's operational procedures.

The school grounds

Numerous favorable interactions transpire within the realm of academia. The aspect that presents greater difficulty is the process of aligning with one another's post-graduation aspirations. However, if you are able to successfully navigate this undertaking, it indicates a profound commitment to a lasting relationship, and the remarkable anecdotes that will be forged from this experience will undoubtedly endure for many years.

On the train

Why don't you encounter someone during your commute from work?

Perhaps it will be the individual engrossed in reading a book adjacent to your location, or the compassionate individual who selflessly relinquishes their seat for a pregnant woman, or even the individual whose hand inadvertently grazes against yours while gripping the pole by the entrance. In the event that these objects lack elegance, there is a potential risk of them descending upon you in the event of an unforeseen jolt on the train. However, such an incident would undoubtedly furnish an splendid anecdote for future recollections.

Streets

A close acquaintance once recounted to me a splendid encounter he had with a lady. He extended a gesture to lend her his umbrella, recognizing the inclement weather and her lack of one. They indulged in a fleeting yet indelible romantic encounter, and a comparable circumstance could manifest itself in your own existence. Not all individuals whom we encounter possess benevolent motives, but should the act appear sincere and permissible, permit the camaraderie to progress.

Experiencing congestion in traffic.

Take a seat in the driver's seat and tune into vocal-intensive talk radio hosts amidst frequently heard songs; one never knows who might be in the adjacent vehicle. A casual acquaintance encountered her significant other under extreme and burdensome traffic conditions that caused vehicles to come to a standstill for several hours. After a certain duration, individuals alighted from their vehicles, as anticipated, consequently leading to her fortuitous encounter with her prospective romantic partner.

It is possible that you have encountered a similar situation when encountering a traffic jam, experiencing a delay on a train or subway, or enduring a protracted bus journey to a different destination. Remain receptive to the potential for remarkable occurrences in circumstances that may not initially appear optimal or romantic.

In an audibly bustling waiting area

Have you had the pleasure of meeting Jessa? May I inquire about the identity of the remarkably fashionable and extraordinarily attractive character featured in Girls? She displays a liberated spirit on the show and has had an exuberant youth in reality, yet the manner in which she encountered her spouse was rather traditional. They encountered each other in the reception area of her physician's establishment, where the initial connection that eventually culminated in their marriage within a year commenced: "I was suffering from bronchitis, and though I am uncertain of his purpose of visit, I admired him immensely and offered him my contact information." For the majority of our four-year relationship, we have been wed. There does not appear to have been a dramatic pursuit or unnecessary psychological turmoil. They established an immediate interpersonal connection, which subsequently led to significant outcomes.

GHOSTING

"Two instances of online dating to provide further elucidation".

I had been in a romantic relationship for nearly two months. Everything appeared to be progressing smoothly—we had arranged to socialize the following weekend. Subsequently, he conveyed via text message that he had to cancel our scheduled engagement owing to his hospitalization. Out of concern, I made multiple attempts to contact him via text and phone calls to inquire about his well-being; however, regrettably, he did not provide a response. I experienced a cyclic interplay of apprehension, bewilderment, and resentment as I grappled with his prolonged absence of eleven days. I eventually sent him a message inquiring, 'Have you departed?' He apprised me of his recent discharge from the medical facility subsequent to an urgent cardiac surgical procedure. I felt awful. I inquired about his well-being and inquired about any ways in which I may be of assistance.

He provided an explanation, expressing his need for a period of recuperation, and assured me that he would reach out to me at the earliest opportunity. Subsequently, I received no further communication from him. I have attempted to establish communication with him through a series of text messages to inquire about his well-being, yet regrettably, I have not received any response. Due to my inability to distinguish between reality and falsehood, it became one of the most exasperating encounters I have ever encountered. Is he intentionally avoiding communication with me due to him being offended by my inquiry regarding his well-being and his fabrication of the surgery narrative solely to provide me with solace? Was the surgery legitimately performed, or was the emotional burden of the relationship insurmountable? I\\\'ll never find out.

YET ANOTHER TALE

We were introduced via a web-based dating application in July of 2017. There was an immediate rapport established, accompanied by a multitude of electronic correspondences. The initial encounter occurred at his residence. We engaged in a lengthy conversation prior to our initial moment of intimacy. He subsequently departed to embark on a journey, in accordance with his frequent practice. Subsequently, following a couple of text exchanges, he abruptly disappeared. I was in a state of distress for several weeks following my initial experience of being abruptly ignored or avoided without explanation. Over time, I gradually moved on from it.

We will encounter each other once more during the spring season of 2019. Notwithstanding my skepticism, he surpasses expectations. He kindly extends an invitation to join him for dinner. Several days later, he paid a visit to my residence to partake in a wine-drinking occasion. Upon the conclusion of his bicycle riding group's activities on Saturday mornings, he proposes that we convene for a rendezvous over a cup of coffee. He frequently visits my residence to prepare meals on my behalf. Approximately three months after our reconnection, he sent me a photograph of himself delivering a presentation at a conference that week, captured aboard the airplane as he returned home temporarily. I have not received any communication from him regarding our planned coffee date on Saturday morning. I sent him a text message at twelve o'clock in the afternoon. I sent him a message via text later in the day." "I communicated with him via text message later on that same day." "I corresponded with him through a text later in the day." "I reached out to him through a text message at a later point during the day.

Regrettably, he encountered an accident involving a car during his morning bike ride on Saturday and unfortunately succumbed to his injuries by late Sunday morning. He remained deafeningly silent. On Monday, I dispatched my concluding message wherein I conveyed my lack of knowledge regarding his whereabouts or survival, along with my expressed desire to withhold any further action until such time when my significance to him merits a response. Subsequently, it was ascertained that he remained alive and he refrained from providing any justifications for his abrupt disengagement.

In Pursuit of Mr. Right: A Tale by a Female Acquaintance

During our childhood, many of us harbor aspirations of encountering our ideal suitor, and as we mature, it becomes apparent that we are consistently in pursuit of this individual. Whether it be within educational institutions, social gatherings, virtual platforms, upscale retail establishments or fitness facilities, the search for a compatible partner persists. I persisted in my search, continuously scouring for a solution. At the time, I was a young adult of twenty, pursuing higher education, and had recently achieved a substantial weight loss, consequently fostering a sense of confidence within me. Individuals approached me, yet none managed to captivate my attention, and I never encountered the enchanting connection or compatibility that I had previously come across in literature.

For an extended duration, I held the gentleman accountable for his perceived lack of humor, intelligence, competence, excessive attractiveness, absence of ambition, inadequate focus on my well-being, and similar deficiencies. I was teetering on the brink of relinquishing my efforts. I contemplated engaging in recreational activities and casual relationships, like many of my acquaintances were pursuing at that period. However, I was unable to forsake my

fundamental ideals and individual moral rectitude in this manner. Conversely, I started to question whether I was implementing an erroneous approach. Could it be feasible that I am seeking in the incorrect locations? Might it be conceivable that you are searching in an incorrect location?

I came to the realization that I possessed a lack of clarity regarding the specific attributes I sought in a prospective partner. I was aware of the aspects I didn't appreciate about him, yet I was so fixated on the drawbacks that I failed to recognize any positive attributes he might have had.

Subsequently, I made the deliberate choice to embark upon a novel undertaking, akin to an introspective and experimental voyage of self-discovery. I consented to accompany anyone who extended an invitation, despite lacking initial physical appeal. This is logical; I relied on my intuition and steered clear of individuals who displayed dubious behavior. I encountered the majority of the individuals through mutual acquaintances, social gatherings, on the university premises, or at the Starbucks café. I exerted considerable effort to maintain a receptive attitude. Due to his boldness in asking me out, I extended him the presumption of innocence.

Over a span of six months, I engaged in the experience of dating approximately seven or eight individuals. Although primarily consisting of initial encounters, there were a few instances in which subsequent meetings occurred. Although I was unable to secure a romantic partner, I gained significant self-awareness and personal growth. A pivotal aspect of my approach entailed approaching each date with a receptive mindset, whereby I sought to glean insights about the individual and remained genuinely inquisitive about my own inclinations and preferences without the preconceived notion of finding an ideal romantic partner. Approaching the encounter with a receptive mindset also facilitated the expression of my genuine self, fostering engaging conversation and joviality. A portion of the stress I had been imposing upon myself had alleviated. I was indifferent to the outcome, regardless of whether it was successful or not. I had aspirations of encountering someone captivating and engaging, yet alas, neither I nor the gentleman were deemed compatible despite our lack of chemistry.

A charming gentleman entered the coffee establishment where I was employed several months subsequent to the conclusion of said experiment. After a few weeks of fulfilling his requests and preparing his double short lattes, he extended an invitation to me. A resurgence of butterflies and anxiousness ensued, most likely attributed to my inclination towards him and my yearning for a successful outcome. Nevertheless, I made a conscious effort to implement the knowledge I had acquired in a universal sense. I maintained a direct and open approach while refraining from any form of criticism or judgment. We had established a resilient bond that endures to this day. I am skeptical that the outcome would have been successful had I not acquired the knowledge that I did.

Discovering Your Compatible Partner: Criteria To Consider When Searching For A Prospective Life Companion

To identify your ideal partner, it is imperative to engage in self-reflection and gain a thorough understanding of the qualities you prioritize. The subsequent phase entails having a clear understanding of the qualities you do not desire in a potential romantic companion. As an illustration, if you have harbored a longstanding aspiration to engage with individuals belonging to a specific racial or ethnic background, it is advisable to accord significant attention to this aspect during your initial inquiry. You should also take into consideration any other preferences that may hold significance to you. Are you seeking companionship from friends or individuals who are unfamiliar to you within the context of this relationship? Are you seeking a partner who shares the same faith? All of these inquiries are ones that you must contemplate.

The subsequent course of action entails obtaining additional insights regarding the essential attributes valued by your ideal partner.

Thus, you have ultimately reached the decision to embrace a committed relationship with the individual who epitomizes compatibility with you. The subsequent phase entails further exploration into the essential attributes that are pertinent to your ideal counterpart.

IDENTIFY WHAT QUALITIES

GO TOGETHER

The initial step involves considering which qualities are coherent. These attributes encompass both physical features and characteristics of one's personality. Frequently, individuals who share similarities in age, stature, mass, and ethnic background tend to experience a mutual attraction. Nonetheless, the union of an amiable individual with an elegant residence can prove to be an exemplary pairing. Allow us to commence by delving into the realm of physical attributes. This is the initial factor that will elicit your interest in an individual. Gaining insight into your preferences in a partner will aid you in establishing the specific attributes you seek. Beauty: What comprises the allure of an individual?

In general, individuals tend to perceive someone as visually appealing if they share similarities in terms of their racial background, physique, and age. This phenomenon commonly occurs due to individuals' tendency to be drawn to those who bear resemblance to their own characteristics. An individual who appears to be compatible will exhibit considerable similarities with you. An individual who appears as a better fitting companion will evoke a sense of self-recognition in you. Typically, individuals who share similar characteristics with oneself tend to evoke a greater sense of attraction.

SO, WHAT\\\'S NEXT? What are the subsequent steps to take following the identification of a compatible partner?

We\\\'ve all been there. You have developed an affectionate interest or a romantic rendezvous, and you have already ascertained their suitability as a life partner. However, what course of action do you currently undertake? Could you please provide guidance on the process of developing a deeper understanding of their character? What qualities or attributes do you seek in a partnership?

Once the exhilarating moment of discovering your ideal partner occurs, the subsequent stage entails transitioning your initial attraction into profound affection. There are measures you can take to ensure synchronization with your partner, preserving harmonious rapport throughout the entirety of your relationship.

1. Know Your Type

The most ideal relationships are those founded on compatibility. Why not ascertain compatibility prior to entering into a romantic partnership? Would it not be advisable to more thoroughly acquaint yourself with an individual prior to embarking on a romantic partnership?

If you have engaged in several outings with an individual, it is likely that you have been able to ascertain whether or not they are the appropriate match for you. You may have already established a viewpoint regarding their compatibility with you. If you are undecided regarding the suitability of their propositions, I urge you to invest a brief moment in acquainting yourself with your own preferences.

The primary factor driving this phenomenon is the phenomenon of love being devoid of rational judgment. The emotional state of your partner may not always be readily observable, but your own emotions are within your perceptible range. If you are uncertain about whether or not someone is suitable for you, it is advisable to conduct thorough research to determine their compatibility with you.

2. Take into account their familial background.

Gaining insights into an individual's family background is an invaluable method to discern their character traits and their ability to cope with challenges. In the context of a initial encounter, it is permissible to inquire about the individual's family dynamics, upbringing, and personal life encounters. Although family background should not be considered the sole determinant, it serves as an excellent initial point of reference in assessing compatibility with another person.

3. Consider the Possibility of Embracing the Adverse Outcome

Life is fraught with uncertainties and potential perils. Determining which opportunities are worthwhile can often be challenging, however, contemplating the potential worst-case outcomes could provide some guidance. In the event that you are incompatible with another individual, it is quite effortless for hypothetical situations and negative possibilities to obscure your discernment. Rather than deferring the conversation about the trajectory of your relationship until you have attained a state of commitment, may I suggest contemplating it during the initial stages of your courtship, such as the first date.

4. Do not underestimate the potency of a compelling narrative.

Regardless of whether it pertains to an interesting fact, amusing anecdote, or a matter of greater significance, a well-told narrative consistently serves as an effective means to initiate conversation and establish a comfortable atmosphere. One can gain significant insights about an individual's character by examining their narratives. Thus, by attentively listening and analyzing the stories shared during an initial encounter, one can assess compatibility and determine whether or not this person aligns with their future vision.

5. Embrace your true identity, while refraining from exhibiting disrespectful behavior.

Individuals are drawn to one another based on various factors. Regrettably, on certain occasions individuals may exhibit an inclination towards unsavory characters. What you should strive to prevent is the occurrence of undesirable individuals. If you harbor concerns regarding the prospect of facing judgment, if you possess an indifference towards others' perceptions of your thoughts and actions, or if you simply prefer to refrain from expressing your true essence during the initial encounter, then it is evident that this individual may not align with your values and objectives.

Maintain authenticity and prioritize shared interests or values.

6. Maintain your authentic self, while ensuring it remains balanced and appropriate.

The most effective approach to engaging with new individuals is by behaving authentically. If one excessively indulges in the \"I'm not myself right now\" facade, one is unlikely to derive any enjoyment. Ensure that you are at ease and in command of how you represent yourself.

Cease Your Search For Someone To Love You And Instead Focus On Cultivating Self-Love.

In the opening of this book, I made reference to the void of love within me, which my mother was unable to fulfill due to a lack of understanding. Regrettably, my father, who could have completed the task, was also absent from my side. Furthermore, he demonstrated a lack of initiative in seeking me out during my absence, further exacerbating my perception of being undervalued by him. This experience engendered a sustained animosity within me, leading to enduring struggles with diminished self-esteem over the course of several years.

To address my readers who do not identify with the Christian faith, kindly allow me to reference this scriptural passage in order to emphasize my argument: "One should wholeheartedly devote themselves to adoring the Lord, prioritizing their love for their fellow beings just as they do for themselves." The main focus lies on the aspect of "your own self". One cannot genuinely express love towards their neighbor or anyone else until they have acquired the ability to love themselves foremost. Presented below are some indications that can help determine whether one truly possesses self-love. Take a moment to reflect upon the following inquiries: do you find contentment in embracing your true self? Would you desire to assume the identity of another person? Do you like you?

If one harbors antipathy towards oneself due to dissatisfaction with their physical appearance or stature and fails to conduct themselves with proper care and esteem, it is likely that others will also not extend favorable treatment. Furthermore, this could potentially result in consistently attracting individuals who do not appreciate your worth, exacerbating the situation.

Are you capable of sustaining a solitary existence for a complete day, detached from electronic devices such as a television or mobile phone, or do you frequently rely on external validation to derive a sense of self-worth? Do you continue to hold yourself accountable for certain occurrences in the past, particularly those where you lacked influence or control? If you affirmatively respond to any of these inquiries, it indicates that you possess a diminished sense of self-worth, which could potentially exert an influence upon your person, should it remain unresolved prior to wedlock, my lady.

That was my personal encounter: when I reached the age of 18, I made the decision to enter into a romantic partnership with the intention of fulfilling my yearning to be genuinely loved and comprehended by another individual. Regrettably, I became entangled with an inappropriate partner: he was my initial romantic involvement, considerably older than me, and unbeknownst to me, he was already involved with someone else prior to and during our relationship. He desired to maintain flexibility in his choices, in order to select the most optimal outcome. However, regrettably, he mistreated me and neglected to allocate any consideration towards my needs.

the attention for which I had a pressing need: His communication with me was infrequent and he often claimed to be too busy whenever we managed to talk.

Entering into that relationship exacerbated my troubles. I experienced an inability to consume food or attain restorative rest. The sole instance in which I experienced happiness within that relationship was during the periods in which he was present, and I took on the role of nourishing not only him, but also the relationship itself, as he did not possess a fondness for culinary pursuits.

Upon discovering that he was involved romantically with another individual, I terminated the relationship. I

I had no desire to perish on account of an individual who showed minimal regard for my well-being and merely exploited my presence. As I departed, my happiness was restored: that particular relationship proved to be a source of great torment, my dear gentlemen.

Shortly after the dissolution of said relationship, occurring within a mere two-month span, I promptly entered into a subsequent one due to a lack of comprehension regarding the importance of self-love, independence, and personal happiness without relying on external influences. I failed to afford myself the opportunity for adequate recovery.

Subsequently, I continually embarked on new relationships shortly after parting ways, until eventually reaching the sixth individual. After the dissolution of our previous relationship, it was necessary for me to observe a period of six months before embarking on a subsequent romantic commitment, ultimately culminating in matrimony. The duration of six months provided an invaluable opportunity for extensive introspection and thoughtful contemplation of my true desires and aspirations. I came to the realization that I had not cultivated sufficient self-esteem to discern the suitable individuals to enter into relationships with. Consequently, I indiscriminately accepted advances from any suitor, thereby attracting a wide array of individuals into my life.

After the passage of those six months, I achieved emotional fulfillment, cultivated self-love, and came to the realization that any prospective suitor fortunate enough to enter into matrimony with me would indeed be favored. Until that time, my ideal partner failed to materialize.

Self-esteem is the subjective evaluation of our own worth and value. It pertains to our perception of our own identity and the positive appraisal we give to ourselves. This exerts a significant influence on the formation of our behavior.

The presence of diminished self-worth will exert a notable impact on one's interpersonal connections, as well as their marital bonds.

This brings to mind a married couple who sought therapy in order to enhance their intimate relationship. They were not deriving the same level of pleasure from sexual activity as they desired. Numerous inquiries were posed, and as the proceedings progressed, it became evident that the wife harbored feelings of inadequacy due to her bodily proportions.

This psychological issue exerted an influence on her intimate encounters, causing her to experience feelings of excessive weight and prompting her to consistently ensure the absence of light. Furthermore, it consumed her thoughts during their intimate engagement, thereby impeding her ability to derive pleasure from the experience.

CAUTION: The following guidance is exclusively intended for individuals who are married.

Should you encounter difficulties regarding your intimate relationship within the confines of your marriage, it is advisable to reflect upon the mental engagement you possess during these encounters. By consciously investing your cognitive faculties, you are likely to derive considerable satisfaction from the experience.

Although this was her marriage, her lack of self-confidence impeded her ability to fully experience sexual intimacy with her husband. However, it is not necessary to wait until marriage for these issues to manifest. Begin cultivating a positive self-perception at this present moment.

It has come to my attention that certain individuals may have made various remarks about your physique, such as perceiving you as thin, overweight, or lacking in height. If I may interject my own observation, I have noticed that individuals of shorter stature tend to exhibit a notable sense of pride and defensiveness, often accompanied by quick-witted responses, which may occasionally manifest in a negative manner. This behavior might stem from a perception that their stature makes them susceptible to being taken advantage of by others. (I beg your pardon, it is simply an observation) However, if this aligns with your personal encounters, I would humbly offer a straightforward counsel: your sense of value should not be derived from external opinions, but rather should be cultivated from within, nourished by your inherent essence and based on the teachings and guidance provided by a higher spiritual authority. Is the microphone sufficiently loud?

You may have possibly received comments suggesting that you are excessively thin, overly dark-skinned, excessively overweight, or lacking in adequate physical attractiveness. Inform them that "it aligns with my intentions and I have been blessed with good health by a higher power." Your ideal partner will admire and appreciate you for who you truly are, as personal preferences vary significantly from one individual to another, making it evident that we all possess unique tastes.

In the past, there was a prevailing cultural preference for thinness and it was widely promoted as the ideal beauty standard. However, currently, there is a shift towards appreciating a curvier physique that is well-proportioned, which has become fashionable. Even the men

No one is excluded; previously, the configuration consisted of six packs, whereas now it comprises seven packs. See? Regardless of your appearance, embrace your uniqueness and cultivate self-love.

However, if necessary, you can also augment your appearance.

When discussing the enhancement of one's appearance, it is important to clarify that I am not referring to procedures such as buttocks and bust enlargement. These methods can result in numerous adverse effects, some of which may be quite severe. Surely, you must have heard of the potential risks associated with such techniques, including instances of complications arising over time. Regardless of the size of your buttocks, it is essential to acknowledge that your ideal partner will hold great admiration for them.

In my family, we embody transparency, evident through our honesty and integrity. Additionally, we possess a pleasing physique, characterized by well-proportioned features in the appropriate areas. During my youth, I aspired to possess a conventional physique, leading me to consume copious amounts of limewater in an attempt to shed weight. Additionally, I would purposely adorn oversized apparel to render my physique less noticeable. That was until I underwent a rigorous six-month process of self-rehabilitation. Following this, I developed a deep appreciation for my physique and began selecting clothing that flattered it rather than revealing it. When my ideal partner first encountered my image, he silently beseeched that I possessed attractive lower limbs. On the day we met, he expressed great satisfaction upon discovering that I did indeed have this feature. He clasped my hands for an extended period of over thirty minutes during our shared stroll. *Winks

An instance of beauty enhancement that could be considered is if there was an incident during your early adulthood wherein your teeth became damaged, resulting in an unsightly appearance whenever you smile. However, it is worth noting that there are measures that can be taken to address this matter. Alternatively, the shade of your teeth may be a factor, and you have the option to choose teeth whitening as a solution.

It is possible that your legs exhibit a condition such as bowing or being k-legged, potentially resulting in a distorted appearance. It may be worthwhile to address this matter, particularly if aesthetic concerns are involved. Physical activity can contribute to improving your physique and building muscle definition. Similarly, your hair may also differ in length as not everyone possesses long hair. If you come across a hair growth product that proves effective, it would be advisable to make a purchase. Regularly choose a hairstyle that suits your features, maintain a balanced and nutritious diet, ensure an ample intake of water, and diligently attend to the needs of your skin. Radiate confidence! Admire and appreciate yourself each day.

Single but not lonely

Indeed, being single does not necessarily equate to experiencing feelings of loneliness. Another facet of cultivating self-love involves embracing and cherishing your period of singleness: It should not be regarded as a detrimental or unlawful state, but rather as an essential stage for unveiling one's true purpose. Many unattached individuals tend to experience apprehension during this particular phase, particularly if it endures for an extended duration. Do not fret, as I once shared a similar experience. Rest assured that you are not alone in this, but I kindly implore you to refrain from succumbing to despair.

During the phase of singularity, individuals have the opportunity to nurture their character and cultivate self-assurance, allowing for the acquisition of vital skills in collaborative living. If you are an unmarried individual who is prepared for matrimony and continues to reside with your parents, it is advisable to relocate.

Commence strategizing for your transition to independent living and cultivate self-reliance, as failure to undertake this endeavor may result in undue dependency upon your partner. One might anticipate that the gentleman would exhibit similar behavior towards you as your parents did, and if this does not transpire, it is possible that you may develop a perception that he harbors no affection for you, which may be an inaccurate sentiment.

Acquaint yourself with the practice of coexisting with a familial individual whom you were previously unacquainted with, and you will gain significant insights into your own self. One might inquire, "What if I resided independently during my academic years?" However, the circumstances differ; an individual ought to be employed and sustain financial autonomy. During your academic tenure, you relied upon your parents for financial means and necessities; however, this present circumstance marks a distinct departure from that scenario.

Do not harbor fear of solitude for a temporary period; rather, ensure that you do not succumb to a sense of isolation and desolation. Do not derive your self-worth solely from receiving compliments from others, as this can lead to immense emotional distress when those compliments cease or are replaced with insults. Such prolonged anguish may have adverse effects on your chances of finding a suitable partner.

Derive your self-esteem from the understanding that you are intricately and deliberately formed. As a woman, you have been meticulously crafted by a higher power, with every feature of your body tailored to serve your unique purpose. Your nose, lips, and hair have been fashioned with intention, and the man who is meant for you will effortlessly embrace and adore them.

chapter 2

Important considerations about oneself to take into account prior to embarking on the quest for a compatible life partner.

According to relationship expert Dr. Venessa Marie Perry, being aware of these aspects of oneself prior to entering into a relationship can greatly contribute to a more fulfilling romantic partnership. This self-awareness not only fosters effective communication with one's partner but also prevents potential conflicts from arising. Self-awareness will also enable you to remain focused on attaining the exact fulfilment and necessities from your partner, whilst concurrently shielding you from becoming entangled in detrimental situations. Herein lie a few crucial aspects that merit your knowledge and contemplation before embarking upon a new relationship.

1. Desired Attributes in a Romantic Partnership

Prioritize establishing a well-defined set of qualities that characterize your ideal company, prior to venturing into the realm of professional partnerships. "The commencement of a new relationship is a remarkable phase, and it can be easy to get immersed in the moment and lose sight of one's personal aspirations and the collective goals of the relationship," states Alice Roberts, licensed clinical social worker and mental health coach at Wasatch Family Therapy. Having well-defined goals can help maintain your focus on finding a partner who can actively participate in pursuing them alongside you.

2. Regardless

In light of this, it will be necessary for you to address all significant matters. Would you consider dating an individual who smokes? Is it not your desire to have children? What are your thoughts on dishonesty and academic misconduct? "If you fail to communicate your significant concerns and remain oblivious, you may inadvertently jeopardize your true desires and necessities," affirmed Dr. Susan Golicic, a relationship coach, while speaking to Bustle.

3. What is the specific type of 'connection style' that you possess?

Roberts informs me about various distinct types of attachment styles, such as "avoidant," characterized by consciously avoiding one's significant other, and "restless," which entails seeking continuous reassurance from one's partner. In addition, it is highly prudent to acquire a thorough comprehension of one's inherent capabilities before embarking upon any collaborative endeavors. Examining previous relationships to identify areas of vulnerability can aid in taking proactive steps towards building a resilient foundation in future relationships."

4. In the event that you are prepared for a relationship.

When transitioning out of a prolonged or intimate partnership, it is acceptable to grant yourself a period of time prior to embarking on a new one. According to certified coach Anza Goodbar, it is important to allocate time to recover and evaluate the reasons behind the failure of your previous relationship.

Allocate dedicated periods for introspection to examine your personal contribution to the termination of the former friendship, and identify behaviors that contributed to conflicts or dissatisfactions resulting in the breakdown of the relationship. This will enable you to refrain from engaging with these behaviors in future encounters.

5. Your Degree of Self-Value

It is prudent to cultivate your sense of self-value, encompassing confidence, fearlessness... Whatever term you wish to designate it as, it is important to establish this prior to embarking on a relationship. According to Goodbar, establishing a healthy relationship becomes a challenge when one lacks self-respect. Assess the qualities and attributes you contribute to the relationship and maintain a confident outlook regarding your ability to contribute to the growth and advancement of an emerging romance.

6. Regardless

Concurrently, it is advisable to be aware of both your limitations and any associated deficiencies that you may contribute to the partnership. "Prepare yourself to conduct a thorough self-evaluation of your areas of weakness and establish a plan to foster greater equilibrium," suggests Goodbar. For instance, if you do not excel in handling challenges, it would be advisable to develop proficiency in conflict resolution, demonstrating a firm sense of reassurance while avoiding reactive responses. By implementing these strategies, your relationship has the potential to significantly improve.

7. Regardless of whether you possess introverted or extroverted tendencies

It is within the realm of possibility to establish and maintain a successful relationship with any combination of considerate or extroverted tendencies. Nevertheless, it is imperative that you still consider the category to which you belong. Individuals who prefer solitude tend to engage in independent introspection, requiring undisturbed periods of solitude throughout the day. In group settings, the energy levels tend to diminish. According to Dr. Ty Belknap, a life mentor, individuals who are socially active tend to engage in remote processing, often reflecting on their thoughts. This data will provide you with valuable insights for navigating any social situations you find yourselves in, ensuring the happiness of both you and your significant other.

8. Your intended allocation of funds

Given that financial matters can significantly impact the outcomes of a relationship, it is advantageous to possess thorough understanding of the valuable contributions one can bring. According to certified financial planner Lucas Casarez, in correspondence with Bustle via email, recognizing and understanding your financial values can aid in effectively managing shared finances as a relationship progresses towards a serious commitment.

9. Preferences and Dislikes Regarding Intimate Encounters

Your intimate relationship is undoubtedly a continuous source of personal growth and learning. However, it is of utmost importance that you possess the capacity to articulate your preferences and requirements within the realm of intimate encounters. "Our sexual satisfaction should not impose a burden on another individual – we aspire to collaborate with our partner in discovering how to please each other, which entails understanding our preferred types and locations of physical touch, as well as recognizing which sexual activities are more likely (or less likely) to lead us to orgasm," declares Sarah Hunter Murray, Ph.D., a sex therapist and relationship expert, in conversation with Bustle. Furthermore, it is imperative to be aware of and respect your personal boundaries in matters of sexual activity. Identifying the specific sexual exercises that make you feel uncomfortable and exploring the reasons behind this discomfort can be both enlightening and empowering. This information can bring about positive developments in your sexual journey.

10. If and when you are willing to make concessions

Enter into a relationship with a thorough awareness of your significant concerns and personal boundaries. Nevertheless, keep in mind that your associate will be engaging in similar actions. Therefore, although it is imperative not to compromise on matters of personal significance, it may be prudent to occasionally reassess one's decisions. Would you truly reconsider this matter? Would it be possible for us to reach an agreement or understanding at any juncture? "Should you fail to exhibit flexibility or carefully deliberate upon the opportunity afforded by time, it may imply an inadequate readiness for the associated responsibilities," advised Davida Rappaport, an esteemed clairvoyant and profound guide.

11. What is Your Desired Career Trajectory

According to Rappaport, it is highly advisable to enter into a relationship with a clear understanding of how you envision your long-term career aspirations unfolding. A strong bond and a chosen professional path can be closely intertwined, and it is indeed possible to navigate these aspects during a romantic courtship. Taking all factors into account, the greater extent to which you are able to plan and establish your career beforehand, the less susceptible you will be to being distracted as time progresses.

12. The optimal approach to attentively heed your intuition.

The ability to be mindful of your physical sensations, particularly regarding digestion, is paramount in social settings, including romantic relationships. "Establishing a robust connection and learning to trust one's innate intuition can serve as a source of strength," stated Angela Lenhardt, a spiritual life coach, in an interview with Bustle. Your intuition may guide you to both open and close doors. The initial stages of a new relationship are always characterized by novelty and excitement. Being attuned to how your instinct specifically assesses the situation can potentially save you a significant amount of time, financial resources, and emotional distress in the future by determining whether the relationship is destined or not.

The individual must strive to cultivate a deeper understanding of the inherent apprehension and aversion associated with establishing close personal connections.

Attending to Our Internal Expert

The linguistic nature of our protection framework and our concern regarding proximity is shared by both doctors. Robert and Lisa Firestone frequently refer to what is commonly known as the 'fundamental internal voice.' People safeguard themselves and their fears by harboring an antiquated, negative self-image, perceiving themselves as morally repugnant or unworthy of establishing a fulfilling relationship. According to Dr. Lisa Firestone, there is a collective presence of "fundamental inner voices" within individuals that inform us when we are deemed excessively overweight, unattractive, aged, or different. When we give heed to these "voices," we engage in behaviors that alienate individuals.

When embarking on a romantic relationship or even contemplating one, our minds tend to be inundated with pessimistic, undermining thoughts about ourselves, as well as critical and doubtful thoughts about others. These 'voices' exemplify a perspective towards self-perception that is often ingrained during formative periods. It seems like one could benefit from the advice of refraining from going out this evening. You\\\'re excessively bashful. You are likely to experience a sense of embarrassment and disappointment. It elicits responses such as asserting that you are unworthy. No one in this vicinity even took notice of your presence. It resurges with a cautionary reminder that you will never encounter someone of your liking. Individuals often disappoint us in various ways. The purpose of this perspective is to hinder our progress, encouraging us to remain complacent within our comfort zones and succumb to fear. Regardless, when it appears defensive, it impedes our ability to assertively seek what we require.

Being Fastidious

Our safeguards can evoke a sense of heightened discernment, albeit not in a positive or self-assured manner, but rather in a more negative and confining fashion that may prompt us to fixate on and magnify the shortcomings of the people we encounter. Our intrinsic thoughts and feelings are not solely directed towards ourselves, but extend to individuals towards whom we may feel an attraction. For certain individuals, these voices manifest persistently in every situation. "She seems to possess an abundance of clarity. " "He appears to potentially lack financial resources." "She will become excessively passionate. " "He is most likely uninteresting." For certain individuals, these notions arise when they begin to feel a closer connection with someone. Maybe we should exercise caution. " "She is not merely remarkable. " "He requires a considerable amount of attention. " The fastidious manners we develop towards a partner or potential partner may impede our ability to be receptive and truly get to know someone. Additionally, the attributes that tend to repel us occasionally prove to be the very qualities we desire or that would bring us contentment. For instance, if a partner displays an excessive affection towards us or is overly warm, we often perceive these traits negatively. It is crucial to contemplate the origins of our fussiness and acknowledge the potential opportunities we may be dismissing by heeding our inner instincts.

2. Your Dream Woman Project

Exhibiting qualities of an idealized woman does not entail conforming to the unrealistic standards exemplified by a Barbie doll. It pertains to embodying a sense of equilibrium within oneself, and endeavoring to enhance one's emotional and physical welfare continuously.

The narrative of Maggie effectively exemplifies the importance of prioritizing personal growth before embarking on the pursuit of securing and maintaining a lifelong romantic partnership.

Maggie embodies an elegant blend of charm, empathy, intellect, and physical allure. However, above all else, her most salient trait is an acute awareness and responsiveness towards the emotions and needs of those around her. The relationship between her parents was characterized by numerous challenges, which greatly impacted Maggie. She desired companionship with an individual who possessed entirely dissimilar qualities to those exhibited by her father. For Maggie, this entailed securing a consistently considerate and empathetic partner. These qualities epitomized the foundations of a successful romantic relationship for her.

She encountered Dave during her twenties. Dave possessed a remarkable combination of attractive physical features, intellectual acuity, and a delightful sense of humor. He was an extrovert. Additionally, he possesses a highly volatile disposition. Contrarily, he possessed a genuine understanding of the importance of family, accountability, and deference.

Following a period of courtship lasting several years, they entered into matrimony and subsequently welcomed the arrival of a baby girl. Maggie admitted to me that they engaged in perpetual conflicts. The relationship continued to deteriorate on a daily basis.

Ultimately, when her daughter reached the age of five, Maggie reached her breaking point and made the decision to depart from her spouse.

Prior to their marriage, she expressed a sense of unease. Nevertheless, she entered into matrimony with him on account of his amiability, as well as her desire to vacate her residence.

Initially, she failed to heed her inner conscience. Dave was not the epitome of what she had envisaged in a prospective life companion, and she was acutely aware of this fact. Maggie perennially desired a gentleman who would exhibit extraordinary kindness and compassion towards her while safeguarding her delicate emotions. That represented the opposite of how her father was. This profound longing has plagued her continuously, impeding her ability to cultivate a fulfilling romantic partnership as she has reached maturity.

This sets an unhealthy precedent for individuals. It would be an implausible feat for any man to consistently exhibit immense kindness, niceness, and attentiveness towards her. It is beyond the capacity of any man to meet her expectations. Consequently, she devoted a significant portion of her life to transitory romantic involvements. Presently, she has reached the age of sixty-five. Regrettably, she failed to grasp the importance of focusing on self-improvement as a prerequisite for attracting and maintaining a romantic relationship.

As it so transpires, I am also acquainted with Dave. In the aftermath of his separation from Maggie, he crossed paths with Lucy, an intelligent and vivacious woman, who derives immense pleasure from her spouse's lighthearted and playful nature. Despite his occasional difficult nature, Lucy understands that she is not accountable for Dave's behavior, and subsequently asserts her authority when necessary. Maggie and she are complete opposites. She has consistently displayed a lack of concern for a man attending to her spiritual wellbeing. She attends to her own well-being and expresses her viewpoints confidently. That is a quality which Dave holds in high esteem and greatly admires. Dave and Lucy have an exemplary bond.

The success of Lucy's relationship with Dave can be attributed neither to her efforts to transform him nor to his inherent growth triggered solely by his association with Lucy. In fact, he presented himself the same way he did when he was with Maggie.

Dave and Lucy constituted an exceptionally versatile and proficient partnership. They experienced adverse experiences during their formative years and faced heartbreak in romantic relationships, however, they demonstrated remarkable resilience and developed enhanced emotional fortitude.

Another noteworthy aspect associated with them is their exceptional ability to maintain their expectations at a reasonable level. They possess a practical and down-to-earth approach.

Exercise caution in establishing the standards and aspirations for your interpersonal partnership. This will result in a substantial reduction in the amount of time spent grappling with confusion and experiencing disappointment.

Each individual possesses a personal history that may have influenced their convictions. On occasion, these convictions manifest as an all-consuming preoccupation that transcends comparison. You possess the ability to actualize your ideal self, becoming the epitome of the woman you aspire to be.

In order to embody the ideal woman, one must maintain a mental disposition characterized by optimism and positivity. It pertains to one's perception and cognitive evaluation of oneself. Undoubtedly, the inherent dreaminess that characterizes you emerges intrinsically.

Regardless of your relationship status, it is imperative that you experience a sense of enchantment. Not only will this serve to draw suitable individuals towards you, but it will also contribute to your overall feeling of well-being.

The dictionary defines dreamy as "a state of mind or experience characterized by whimsical and lovely qualities." It possesses exceptional, unparalleled, or remarkable attributes"... Have you taken note that this is unrelated to your physical appearance, accomplishments, possessions, or others' perception of you?

It can be postulated that some women may find it arduous to internalize their own desirability due to the influence of their past experiences and the implications derived from such encounters. The burden they carry can be quite substantial at times, and the incessant thoughts that occupy their minds consistently contradict the truth. However, I kindly request that you take a moment to reflect on the fact that the past has already elapsed.

The strength of your past lies solely in your willingness to grant it power. It is advisable to frequently revisit and cherish the positive recollections from your past and allow them to shape your present experiences.

You possess the ability to consciously shape your thoughts and cultivate a belief system that aligns with your desired perception. Should you aspire to perceive yourself as an exemplary woman, you will develop the belief and conviction to that effect.

There exists a substantial body of scientific literature that supports the notion that our brain possesses the ability to undergo neural rewiring. If an individual maintains a sustained positive mindset, their cognitive faculties will actively contribute to its enrichment.

Regrettably, the identical holds true when considering the opposite end of the spectrum. If an individual maintains a persistent negative mindset, their brain will readily assume control, thereby contributing to its amplification. It all begins with the internal discourse that one engages in. Please make an effort to maintain a demeanor that is courteous, optimistic, and receptive.

To illustrate the mechanics behind the process of altering one's thoughts and beliefs, one can contemplate an individual endeavoring to improve their physical fitness. The duration and exertion necessary to achieve the objective are contingent upon an individual's initial position.

If one finds themselves in a state of significant physical deconditioning, implying that they do not perceive themselves as an ideal embodiment of attractiveness, it will be necessary to exert additional effort during the initial stages of improvement. Over time, one can achieve a remarkable level of physical fitness. The unwavering determination, resolute perseverance, and unwavering fortitude you display will culminate in a transformation of your convictions.

You will ultimately come to believe in yourself and recognize your authentic essence as an ideal woman. In addition to embodying the ideal partner of your dreams, maintain the belief that you are the object of someone's aspirations. Reiterate daily: I am a woman who embodies the dreams of someone, as surely a man of your dreams is in search of you.

I contend that each woman possesses an inherent tendency towards reverie, yet an element from their personal history has impeded their capacity to exhibit their authentic essence.

There is a significant degree of apprehension surrounding the discovery and expression of one's true identity. Do not permit fear to hinder your pursuit of happiness. The environment has a lasting impact on individuals throughout their lifetimes. This enables us to adapt ourselves and revise the norms to align more effectively with our surroundings and various circumstances, fostering a sense of integration and harmony.

Have you ever come to the realization of how significantly your social environment impacts your actions and behaviors? We collectively exhibit a tendency to adapt on a subconscious level. Does your social milieu exhibit a prevailing sense of pessimism? Is it optimistic? What is it like?

It is advisable to actively seek the company of individuals who possess a positive mindset and consistently align their thoughts with their actions. Exercise caution around individuals who employ pleasant speech while their true intentions and actions diverge significantly.

It is imperative that there exists alignment between the words uttered and actions taken, predominantly in the majority of circumstances. The individual is not required to be flawless, only to exhibit coherency.

Discover sources of inspiration, for it is through these that the potent power to instigate change can be harnessed. After obtaining your inspiration, it is imperative to establish a clear objective, diligently commit yourself to your pursuit, exhibit patience, and derive satisfaction from the entire process.

No obstacle impedes a determined woman who has set her mind on achieving a specific goal and diligently pursues it. One additional catalyst for transformation is profound despair. You are not obligated to commence from that point, however, in circumstances of great distress, you may perceive it as a source of motivation that propels actualization of the desired transformation.

Numerous individuals who have achieved success in matters of love, life, and business have initiated their journeys from a state of profound desperation. The aforementioned individuals were spurred by a sense of urgency, which served as the impetus for them to elevate their efforts, diligently seek solutions, persevere unwaveringly, and ultimately accomplish feats that were once inconceivable.

It is imperative to establish and shape your ideal life well in advance of encountering your prospective life partner, referred to as the "winner." One can attain this objective through proper preparation, self-awareness, understanding one's goals, and most importantly, having a clear plan of action.

Love Yourself Unconditionally

To be beloved by others, it is imperative that we prioritize the cultivation of a positive relationship with ourselves.

Do you love yourself? Really?

Several years ago, during a therapy session with my hypnosis therapist, I experienced profound emotional distress when confronted with the stark truth that I lacked self-love. My emotional response was akin to that of an infant, as tears streamed down my face. I have faced considerable challenges throughout my early adulthood, enduring repeated emotional distress in the context of romantic relationships, where I have experienced instances of infidelity, exploitation, and verbal mistreatment, among other forms of harm.

However, within that fleeting moment, it dawned upon me that the crux of the matter revolved around my own deficiency in self-affection. I have allowed numerous undesirable incidents to transpire in my life, and I have permitted myself to be subjected to mistreatment. The overwhelming sense of profound remorse, shame, and a profound awareness of the pain I have inflicted upon myself caused me to weep even more vehemently.

Please RESPOND to the following statements by indicating whether they are TRUE or FALSE:

I lack the ability to refuse requests and decline the demands of others.

I find it challenging to fulfill both the role of a giver and receiver.

I permit others to mistreat me.

I have unwavering love and profound respect for myself under all circumstances.

I would prefer not to be in solitude.

I consistently engage in self-criticism.

I am unable to fully embrace and appreciate myself entirely.

I believe that others surpass me in capability.

If you have responded affirmatively to any of the aforementioned statements, I regret to inform you that it will be necessary for us to dedicate effort towards enhancing your self-esteem.

Many individuals dedicate significant portions of their lives yearning for affection, eagerly awaiting the arrival of love itself, a person who can bring us fulfillment and prevent us from feeling devoid and aimless in its absence. Nevertheless, the prioritization should be reversed, beginning with self-love.

Cultivating self-compassion entails fostering a deep sense of reverence and affection towards ourselves, which originates from our inner being. When we cultivate this profound self-love, it radiates outward, enveloping others in its embrace.

In the absence of self-love, individuals seek external outlets to fulfill this emotional deficit, be it through companions, pets, or material possessions. Subsequently, we shall promptly ascertain that these fail to meet our desired level of satisfaction, thereby inciting a sense of discontentment or even disillusionment on our part once more.

Are you among the individuals who possess an inclination to never decline requests made by others? Typically, individuals who exhibit this behavior harbor an inherent belief and underlying apprehension. This behavior may stem from a profound aversion towards the prospect of individuals disliking you, leading to a tendency to excessively seek approval and conform to the desires of others, consequently neglecting your own personal needs in the process. When one exerts diligent efforts to meet the expectations of others and seeks their approval by acquiescing to every request, at the detriment of one's own well-being, it can be argued that this behavior does not align with self-love. Inevitably, this approach often leads to exhaustion due to the demands placed by others, and may result in engaging in activities that do not bring personal satisfaction, creating a sense of being coerced or obligated to comply. By performing an action solely out of duty, you are actually providing no benefits to either yourself or the other party involved.

My significant other is an exceptional individual with an insatiable thirst for knowledge and a passion for venturing into uncharted territories. I deeply appreciate his inclination towards exploration and am highly thankful for the opportunity to venture into uncharted territories that would have otherwise remained inaccessible to me without his companionship.

Several years ago, we embarked on a journey to the beautiful mountainous terrain of Himachal Pradesh in India. The entirety of northern India is exquisitely captivating, brimming with ceaseless rivers, majestic mountains, cascading waterfalls, and an array of remarkably charming individuals. Given the enchanting surroundings abundant with natural beauty, it is only fitting that our inclination leads us towards embarking on explorations and indulging in our shared passion for hiking.

Herein lies the disparity between us. I originated from the urban locality, and despite my fondness for hiking, I derive the most satisfaction from undertaking treks characterized by accessible trails featuring well-maintained pathways and minimal inclinations.

On a certain day, we embarked on a leisurely stroll and encountered a pathway that led us to a junction of commerce and a picturesque cascade. I desired to proceed on our current trajectory, despite my partner proposing to venture up a hillside whose ultimate destination remained uncertain, driven by their curiosity about its potential outcome. There is a lack of designated pathway or any infrastructure leading up the hill, necessitating our need to navigate through the densely vegetated area of bushes in order to proceed. I readily acquiesced to his request, observing his evident enthusiasm for exploring the hill, despite my internal reluctance. I desired to bring him joy.

In summary. Throughout the entirety of the walk, I experienced a profound sense of anger, to the point where I found no enjoyment in even a single moment. Adding to the exacerbation, a torrential downpour ensued, compelling us to abort our ascent halfway and descend. The entire area was coated with a treacherously slick surface, and my vision became obscured due to the precipitation obstructing my sight. There came a moment when the challenges became exceedingly arduous, prompting me to lower myself and succumb to tears.

We engaged in a disagreement, and I held him responsible for leading us to this course of action. He was taken aback to discover that I lacked the initial inclination to undertake it. Upon reflection after my emotional state had subsided, it became apparent to me that this entire episode could have been avoided had I remained authentic to my own desires and effectively communicated my limitations and boundaries. I pondered why I had not communicated my initial lack of interest to him, and I resolved to take measures to avoid similar situations in the future.

Indeed, within the context of a relationship, it is imperative to engage in compromise. However, it is essential to discern between wholeheartedly compromising on every aspect and maintaining the ability to compromise while upholding a sense of self-love. When we possess self-compassion, we establish appropriate limits, assert our autonomy, and exhibit the ability to decline others' requests. We possess the ability to engage in simultaneous giving and receiving. We uphold self-respect, extend courtesy towards others, and are well aware of the manner in which we should be treated by others. Similar to how we advocate for our closest companions when we observe them being mistreated, it is equally imperative that we advocate for ourselves in situations necessitating such action.

The sharing of love is perhaps the most profound and exquisite phenomenon that one can encounter in the journey of existence. However, love cannot be shared unless we are consumed by love. When individuals engage in the cultivation of self-compassion, they convey to the cosmic forces their inherent value and worthiness.

The paramount bond that we possess is the one we establish with our own selves. Should we err in our own internal assessments, our interactions with others will invariably be flawed. In cultivating self-love, we assume accountability for our actions, decisions, and the resultant consequences.

Prioritize self-care and self-love as a foundational aspect of your well-being. Cultivate a strong and supportive relationship with oneself. Hold deep affection and embrace your true self unconditionally. By exhibiting such behavior, you will elicit reciprocal treatment from others, mirroring the way you regard and value yourself.

Self-care encompasses more than just personal interests.

It commences with one's own action, in order to foster a robust collective.

~ Exercise ~

Please recite the following phrase audibly on three separate occasions: "

I hereby eradicate and nullify any and all areas within myself where I do not harbor absolute love and acceptance, transcending all chronological, spatial, tangible, and intangible realms instantaneously.

How can I cultivate a state of unwavering self-love and self-acceptance throughout every moment?

Please enumerate the occasions during which you have exhibited an insufficiency in self-affection. Possible rephrasing in a more formal tone: Possible causes may include excessive food consumption, insufficient physical activity, susceptibility to exploitation by others, or any other conceivable contributing factors.

Please compose a statement of forgiveness directed towards yourself for each of the items you have recorded.

For instance, in the case of excessive consumption of food, one can express forgiveness towards oneself by stating, "I acknowledge and pardon myself for engaging in overeating, and I am wholeheartedly open to fully embracing my being at this moment." Complete the blank spaces in the underlined text. One illustration may involve "engaging in self-care practices that show a lack of self-compassion."

On any occasion in your existence wherein you become aware of self-criticism or unfavorable self-assessments, kindly recollect this declaration and peruse it once more.

Please document the actions you can undertake in order to showcase self-care in each of these situations. Reflect upon the question, "If I genuinely possess self-love, what actions would I undertake?"

Kindly transcribe the following statement and proceed to vocalize it: "At this current juncture, I wholeheartedly embrace and cherish myself without any conditions or reservations." Please continue to iterate this practice until such time as you genuinely experience its truth. You may choose to reiterate this affirmation on a daily basis.

In the event that you find yourself facing a circumstance where you are grappling with choices or experiencing a predicament, I urge you to contemplate the question, "If I possess genuine affection for myself, how would I proceed?" Align your daily conduct with the principle of self-care and act accordingly.

Please set aside this book and proceed with the subsequent section tomorrow.

www.ingramcontent.com/pod-product-compliance
Lightning Source LLC
Chambersburg PA
CBHW050418120526
44590CB00015B/2009